# Quest for Kim

*By the middle of the nineteenth century Central Asia was rarely out of the headlines, as one by one the ancient caravan towns and khanates of the old Silk Road fell to Russian arms. Every week seemed to bring news that the hard-riding Cossacks, who spearheaded each advance, were getting closer and closer to India's thinly guarded frontiers. In 1865 the great walled city of Tashkent submitted to the Tsar. Three years later it was the turn of Samarkand and Bokhara, and five years after that, at the second attempt, the Russians took Khiva.*

*Despite St Petersburg's repeated assurances that it had no hostile intent towards British India, and that each advance was its last, it looked to many as though it was all part of a grand design to bring the whole of Central Asia under Tsarist sway. And once that was accomplished, it was feared, the final advance on India – the greatest and richest of all imperial prizes – would begin.*

*The threat seemed real enough at the time, whatever historians may say with hindsight today, for the evidence was there for anyone who cared to look at the map. At the beginning of the nineteenth century, more than 2,000 miles separated the British and Russian empires in Asia. By the end of it, this had shrunk to a few hundred, and in parts of the Pamir region to less than twenty. No wonder many in India and at home feared that the Cossacks would only rein in their horses when India, too, was theirs.*

*From the author's* The Great Game

# QUEST FOR KIM

*In Search of Kipling's
Great Game*

## PETER HOPKIRK

Illustrations by Janina Slater

*Ann Arbor*

### THE UNIVERSITY OF MICHIGAN PRESS

© Peter Hopkirk 1996

First published in the United States of America in 1997
by the University of Michigan Press
Manufactured in the United States of America
⊗ Printed on acid-free paper

2000   1999   1998   1997      4   3   2   1

First published in Great Britain in 1996
by John Murray (Publishers) Ltd.,
50 Albemarle Street, London W1X 4BD

**Library of Congress Cataloging-in-Publication Data**
Hopkirk, Peter.
    Quest for Kim   :   in search of Kipling's great game   /   Peter Hopkirk
;   illustrations by Janina Slater.
        p.   cm.
    ISBN 0-472-10854-9 (cloth)
    1. Kipling, Rudyard, 1865-1936. Kim.  2. Kipling, Rudyard,
1865-1936—Knowledge—India.  3. Kipling, Rudyard, 1865-1936—
Knowledge—Pakistan.  4. English literature—Indic influences.
5. Pakistan—In literature.  6. Orphans in literature.  7. India—In
literature.  8. Spies in literature.  I. Title.
PR4854.K43H67   1997
823'.8—dc21                                                      97-4252
                                                                       CIP

FOR JAMES,
ELIZABETH, VICTORIA
AND TIMOTHY

# Contents

'I have read *Kim* again and again – I do not know
how many times – and taken it on my travels.
It is the only book of prose that I can open at
random, at any page, and read with the same
delight as if it were poetry.'

*Wilfred Thesiger*

'To anyone who has ever lived in India, and
to many who have never set foot in that beautiful,
bewitching, often maddening and sometimes terrifying
land, *Kim* is strong magic.'

*M. M. Kaye*

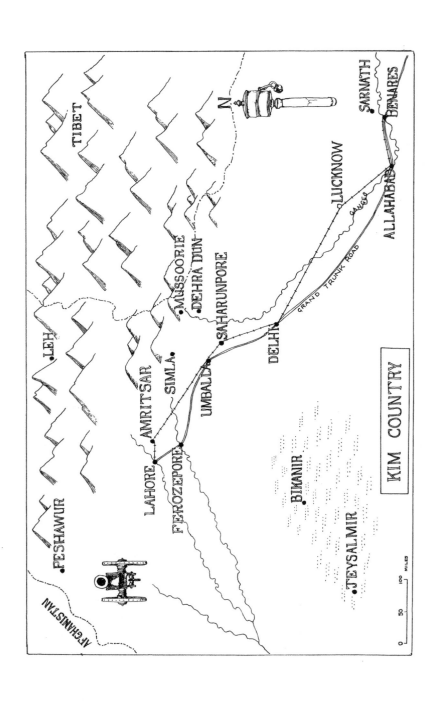

KIM COUNTRY

# 'Here begins the Great Game...'

A GERMAN SNIPER'S bullet, intended to kill a young French officer in the First World War, instead buried itself in a book he was carrying in his breast pocket. It was a French translation of *Kim*. Profoundly grateful, the soldier sent Kipling the badly mauled volume, a hole piercing all but its last twenty pages. Secured to it by a piece of string, threaded through the bullet-hole, was his most precious possession – a Croix de Guerre. He asked Kipling to accept both the book and the medal for thus saving his life, and as a token of his devotion to *Kim*.

After the war Kipling visited the Frenchman and insisted on returning both gifts, arguing that they rightly belonged to the soldier's newly born son. Instead, however, he agreed to become godfather to the boy, christened Jean after Kipling's only son, John, who had been killed in France in 1916 as an eighteen-year-old subaltern in the Irish Guards.

What became of that copy of *Kim*, or of Kipling's young godson, alas is not known.

My own debt to *Kim* is considerably less dramatic than this, although the direction my life has taken owes much to a youthful reading of Kipling's masterpiece. For it was *Kim*, more years ago than I care to remember, which first introduced me to the intoxicating world of the Great Game. To a highly impressionable, romantically minded schoolboy of thirteen – the same age as Kim himself – the mysterious, if murky, activities of men like Colonel Creighton, Mahbub Ali and Lurgan Sahib were heady stuff indeed. This, after all, was at a time when the British still ruled India, and much of the rest of the world, and almost anything seemed possible.

So spellbound was I by this glimpse into the workings of the Indian secret service that I carried a copy of *Kim* everywhere, even if much of it was lost on me. For *Kim*, despite what many people imagine, is not a children's book. Indeed, at the age of thirteen, I was far from certain what the Great Game – 'that never ceases day or night' – was really all about. Nevertheless, it appeared to be something incredibly exciting, and I yearned to discover more. The quest was to last a lifetime, and has still to run its course.

I have since learned that I was far from alone in my attachment to *Kim*. Wilfred Thesiger tells us that he rarely travelled without a copy of it in his saddlebag, while T. S. Eliot read it aloud to his wife in the evenings for the sheer joy of its language. Mark Twain said that he read it afresh every year, while, more recently, Phillip Knightley, the writer on espionage, told me that he too re-reads *Kim* every year, and moreover has named his own son after its young hero. And I once heard Tariq Ali, that one-time scourge of the Establishment, confess that *Kim* was the book he loved most as a boy in Lahore where he, like Kim, was brought up.

Some of today's more adventurous young also appear to be smitten by *Kim*. 'Nothing', one teenage traveller told *The Independent*, 'could ever surpass reading *Kim* while going along the Grand Trunk Road.' She found herself, she confessed, half hoping to encounter a Tibetan holy man and, like Kim, become his *chela*, or disciple. Surprisingly, in view of its imperialist tone, the book has its Indian devotees too. The great Bengali scholar Nirad Chaudhuri has described *Kim* as 'the finest novel in the English language with an Indian theme', and 'great by any standards that ever obtained in any age of English literature'. He admits, however, that he had for years avoided reading it for fear of being wounded by Kipling's well-known dislike of Indian intellectuals, and Bengalis in particular. In fact, one of the book's heroes – Hurree Chunder Mookerjee, or R17 on the Great Game payroll – is a Bengali intellectual, and one of its most lovable characters.

But my own youthful reading of *Kim* did more than simply introduce me to the Great Game. It also opened my eyes to a whole new world, brimming with promise – the mysterious East. The war was not yet over, however, and there was no question of even the most adventurous of teenagers making their way to India. Some twenty years or more were to pass before the hippy trail opened up the East to all comers. My own early forays into the Orient, therefore, had to be much nearer to home. So it was that during the school holidays, while other boys were engaged in more conventional pursuits, I would haunt the little oriental bookshops around the British Museum.

These exotic establishments (or so they seemed to me) were run by erudite-looking men with white hair and central European names. Only one still survives, together with much of its original character, and that is Arthur Probsthain in Great Russell Street, founded in 1902, the year after *Kim* was published, and still frequented by scholars from all over the world. The rest, unhappily, are all long gone. But here I would pore over learned-looking tomes, understanding little or nothing of their contents, but convinced that somehow, by osmosis perhaps, I would absorb some of their secrets.

Among my fellow browsers in these shops were individuals who, I was utterly convinced, must be on Colonel Creighton's payroll. Of scholarly mien, and often of swarthy countenance, these could only be the real-life colleagues of Mahbub Ali, Lurgan Sahib, Hurree Chunder Mookerjee and Kim. In fact, these searchers after knowledge were in all probability professors or their students from the School of Oriental and African Studies, not half a mile away. But to a teenager under the spell of the Great Game that would have been far too simple an explanation. As it turned out, there proved to be an element of truth in these juvenile imaginings, for during the war, I later discovered, the school was used for teaching oriental languages to British intelligence officers.

From the bookshops by the British Museum I would move on to Cecil Court, off Charing Cross Road, where there was a rather dingy little shop which sold oriental antiquities and other eastern artefacts. It was exactly how I imagined Lurgan Sahib's antique shop in Simla to be – that strange establishment where he initiated Kim into the secrets of the Great Game. Here I would gaze covetously at the curious objects in the window, trying to pluck up the courage to enter and ask the grumpy owner, who did not suffer fools at all, least of all young ones, the price of a dented Russian samovar, or some other treasure which had caught my romantic fancy.

In the end I only ever bought one small object, for that was all that my money would run to. This was a brass camel, of the Central Asian kind, bearing a rider on its back and a strange inscription on its base. A seal of some sort, it seemed to me to embody all the allure and excitement of the East. Alas, although the iron gates across the doorway and the well-remembered iron bars on the window still remain, the shop has long since followed its owner into oblivion – but not before a most gruesome murder had taken place among the antiquities in the basement, which only came to light when the body of a young woman was discovered hidden in an ancient Egyptian mummy case there. The little brass camel, however, the only survivor from that early chapter of my life, has fared better, for it sits before me on my desk as I write, its mystic inscription still defying all attempts to decipher it.

At the age of sixteen, still under the fatal influence of *Kim* and Colonel Creighton, and all that they evoked, I set my sights on Sandhurst, determined to join the Indian Army. After all, I reasoned, if I demonstrated the right qualities I might even be picked to play the Great Game – 'that is so large that one sees but a little at a time' – and be sent through the passes into Central Asia disguised as a native horse-trader or Tibetan holy man. Being talent-spotted for the Great Game was, I imagined, rather like being chosen to play wing three-quarter for one's school 1st XV.

Nor, as it happens, was this sporting analogy entirely inappropriate. A Rugby football historian once pointed out to me that Captain Arthur Conolly, the Great Game hero who originally coined that memorable phrase, was a boy at Rugby in the early 1820s when William Ellis first picked up the ball and ran with it. He very likely had that game – and not chess, as is often assumed – in mind when, not long before his execution by the Emir of Bokhara, he wrote to a fellow-player in the Great Game: 'You've a great game, a noble one, before you.' But it was Kipling who pounced on the phrase, some fifty years later, and immortalised it in *Kim*, where he uses it, or some variant of it, no fewer than thirty-six times.

By now it was beginning to dawn even on me that the Great Game was not only over but had been for forty years, and that since then the Russians, far from pouring down through the passes into India, had been our allies in two world wars. Although the Cold War had not yet begun, any remaining dreams I might have had of entering the shadowy, real-life world of *Kim* finally evaporated in 1947 when, after 300 years, the British packed their bags and left India for ever. So ended my adolescent fantasies of single-handedly outmanoeuvring an invading Russian army in the Pamirs and winning a Victoria Cross. But although British India had fallen, to the forces of nationalism rather than to those of the Tsar, the rest of the Empire was still largely intact, with frontiers to be patrolled and guarded. Instead of the Indian Army, therefore, I found myself in Somalia, then under British administration following its seizure from the Italians during the war, serving in the King's African Rifles. I could hardly have been further away from Great Game country – from the North-West Frontier of India, the Pamirs, Afghanistan and Persia, and from Russian and Chinese Central Asia, whose caravan cities and great empty deserts I so yearned to see.

Then, just as I was about to dismiss the Great Game

finally from my life, I stumbled upon another book, newly published, which once more sent the adrenalin racing through me. This was Fitzroy Maclean's *Eastern Approaches*, a brilliantly written account of his pre-war travels and adventures in Central Asia and the Caucasus during the darkest days of Stalin's terror, and his subsequent wartime special missions in Persia and Yugoslavia. It was a classic piece of Great Game writing, albeit about a later game. To a subaltern of nineteen it was heady stuff, for, unlike *Kim*, it was true, and soon I knew parts of it almost by heart. Just as *Kim* had done a few years earlier, *Eastern Approaches* had a powerful and profound effect on me and, I am quite sure, on many of my generation. It read like real-life John Buchan, and perhaps should have carried a health warning, so intoxicating was its cocktail of high adventure and politics. It seems, too, that with the passage of years it has lost none of its potency, for a million copies later it is still in print today.

Reading it made me even more determined to reach Central Asia, preferably pursued, as Maclean himself had been, by Stalin's secret police. Frustratingly, though, it was then a totally closed land. Only after Stalin's death did things gradually, very gradually, begin to get easier. In 1958, at the height of the Cold War, I got to Moscow and Leningrad, but no further. However Fitzroy Maclean, I noticed, managed to return to Central Asia that same year, although it needed Nikita Khrushchev's personal blessing to get him to Bokhara. Alas, I had no such powerful friends in the Kremlin. Indeed, in 1963, when the newspaper I by then worked for applied for a visa for me to be based as a foreign correspondent in

Moscow, this was abruptly refused. No explanation was given, although not long before I had been attacked by name in *Pravda* for investigating covert Soviet activities in Africa, and prior to that had spent a week in a Cuban secret police cell, accused of spying (with, as it happened, only *Kim* to read).

It was thus not until 1968 that I was at last able to visit Central Asia, albeit under rigorous supervision, and gaze, like a million tourists since, at the dazzling blue tiles of Samarkand and the ancient mud-brick mosques of Bokhara. Further forays into Great Game country now followed, with exploratory visits to Khiva, Kashgar, Kabul, outer Mongolia, northern Pakistan and Himalayan India. Wherever possible I tried to track down the precise spots where the most stirring or memorable exploits in the century-long Anglo-Russian struggle had taken place. More often than not this was where some British player in this dangerous game had met his lonely end.

In Bokhara there was the square where, 4,000 miles from home, Colonel Stoddart and Captain Conolly were beheaded in the summer of 1842, and under which their remains almost certainly still lie. In Kabul, somewhere in the old town, can be found the approximate spot where Sir Alexander Burnes was brutally hacked to death by a furious Afghan mob, though by now all traces of it will almost certainly have been obliterated by rocket fire during the recent bloody civil war. In northern Pakistan, near the remote village of Darkot, I tracked down the desolate ravine where in 1870 George Hayward was treacherously murdered while on his way, on a Great Game mission, up into the Pamir passes. There are numerous other such spots which I still hope to find, though time is now no longer on my side. For example, somewhere on the old Karakorum Pass, once the main route from northern India into China, stands a lonely monument to Andrew Dalgleish, a young Scottish player in the Great Game, who was murdered there in 1888. But no one has seen it since 1949, when the last caravan passed that way. For the 19,000-foot pass runs through a bitterly contested border area where, for the past decade, Indian and Pakistani troops have been locked in a bloody stalemate, making it a strictly no-go area.

In addition to exploring the Great Game battlefield, I also read the first-hand narratives of those players, both British and Russian, who left accounts of their adventures and misadventures, as well as the works of contemporary analysts and commentators on Central Asia and the Russian threat to India. Most of these, alas, are now long out of print and impossible to obtain, except from a specialist library or at a very high price. Some, happily, have been reprinted, notably by Oxford University Press, and I have contributed new introductions to a number of these. Finally, over the years, I paid numerous visits to the India Office Library, in London, where I spent fascinating hours studying the secret British archives and intelligence reports of the Great Game era, and the years following the Russian Revolution, when it all began again with a vengeance as Lenin set his sights on India.

All this took up a great deal of time, as it had to be fitted into a career on *The Times*. But by getting up very early –

often at 4.30 a.m. – I managed to write three books on imperial rivalry in Central Asia while still on the staff as a Middle and Far Eastern specialist. It was only when I embarked on the fourth and fifth books – *The Great Game* and *On Secret Service East of Constantinople* – that I decided, very sadly, and after nearly twenty happy years, to leave *The Times* in order to concentrate on book-writing.

By 1994, with the publication of the fifth book, I felt that I had fully exhausted the subject, having finally run out of characters and events of sufficient interest to justify a further book. I also feared that my long-suffering readers might be equally exhausted by the subject. So it was that I found myself turning back to where it had all begun – to *Kim* where, half a century earlier, I had first come across the Great Game. I wanted to discover all I could about the book, its characters, its locations, and how it came to be written. It was strictly a personal quest, and when I embarked on it I had no intention of putting it into a book. Indeed, some may wish that I had stuck to my original resolve, for it is a bold man who believes that he can add anything of value or consequence to Kipling's masterpiece. *Kim* occupies a special place in many people's hearts, not to mention in English literature. Woe betide anyone, therefore, who takes liberties with this deeply loved book, for he risks annoying everyone and pleasing no one, and thus bringing down upon his head the scorn and wrath of half the literate population of Britain.

But not everyone, it should be pointed out, loves *Kim*, or its author. In his day, Kipling's work was much vilified by some critics. One angrily dismissed him as 'an ill-educated, little-brained, second-rate journalist, with all his sickening egotism and vanities'. And as if that was not enough, he went on to attack Kipling's 'smartness and superficiality, jingoism and aggressive cocksureness, rococo fictional types and overloaded pseudo prose'. Few, if any, writers today have to face that sort of abuse, and if they did would probably reach for their lawyer. Yet who has ever heard of Francis Adams, author of *Essays in Modernity*, who thus vented his spleen on Kipling? Or, for that matter, of R. W. Buchanan, who denounced Kipling in his *Voice of the Hooligan* as typifying 'all that is most deplorable, all that is most retrograde and savage'?

More recently both Kipling and *Kim* have become the targets of sanctimonious critics, especially in the United States. Declaring that all of Kipling's writing is 'shot through with hatred', the late American critic Edmund Wilson accused Kim of betraying those, the Indians, whom he 'considered his own people' by delivering them into the bondage of 'the British invaders'. He also accused Kim, by that time aged sixteen, of spurning the advances of the Woman of Shamlegh because she is only a 'native' while he is a sahib. Kipling, he added with perhaps more justification, was 'implacably opposed to every race and nation which has rebelled against . . . the Empire', and to anyone, be they Liberals or Fabians, who dared to question British imperial policy.

More recently still, Professor Edward Said of Columbia University has accused Kipling of racial stereotyping and stigmatising, particularly in *Kim*, objecting, for example, to his observation that 'Kim could lie like an Oriental'. He nonetheless regards *Kim* as 'a work of great aesthetic merit' which 'cannot be dismissed simply as the racist imagining of one fairly disturbed and ultra-reactionary imperialist'. Others, however, are far more hostile, regarding *Kim* as little more than a racist tract. One American academic describes it as 'a complex fantasy of idealised imperialism and colonialism', and Kim himself as an 'emblem of British authority' who is being schooled by Colonel Creighton in 'the strategies of repression'. By rejecting the Woman of Shamlegh's advances, moreover, Kim proves that he has passed 'a crucial test of colonial manhood – the denial of sexuality'. Indeed, if one has not yet read *Kim*, or wishes to enjoy that pleasure again, perhaps one should do so quickly, before the ideologues and zealots of political correctness consign it to the flames, or insist on it being rewritten. Meanwhile the book, now nearly a century old and never once out of print, continues to sell to successive generations of admirers at the rate of nearly 1,000 copies a month, in a number of rival editions and translations.

In the following pages, I have tried to steer clear of such abstractions. My journey into the world of Kim is a purely personal one, and it is particularly the Great Game connections and associations in the narrative which interest me, for it was those which attracted me to the book in the first place. For years I had promised myself that one day I would try to retrace Kim's footsteps across the India of his day, now split between Pakistan and India, and discover how much

of it, if anything at all, remains. Since most of the action in
*Kim* is confined to one small corner of the subcontinent,
this is not exactly a taxing undertaking. Indeed, although I
took longer, it is one which could – at a pinch – be completed
in ten days or so, using modern transport. After all, even
Kim himself covered much of the ground by train, for was
not the railway system one of the great glories of the British
Raj? Most of the events in *Kim*, moreover, occur in easily
identified spots, well known to and vividly described by
Kipling, even if he wrote the book some years after he had
left India for good. It is only when one approaches the
climax of *Kim*, set amid the snowy passes of the Indo-Tibetan
borderlands, that the locations become more blurred and
place names invented.

But although it involves some travel, my account has no
pretensions to being a travel book. Its aim is to explore the
world of Kim and the lama, Colonel Creighton and Lurgan
Sahib, Mahbub Ali and Hurree Chunder Mookerjee. All of
the principal characters in *Kim* were inspired, in whole or
in part, by living individuals, known to or known of by
Kipling when he worked on the *Civil and Military Gazette*
in Lahore from 1882 to 1887, or on the Allahabad *Pioneer*
from 1887 to 1889. The identification of these characters was
as much a part of my quest as were my efforts to pinpoint
the precise locations used by Kipling in his narrative. Indeed,
I spent considerably longer engaged in the former than I did
in exploring Lahore, Umballa (nowadays Ambala), Simla
(now Shimla), the Grand Trunk Road and Saharunpore.
It is hard to say which was the more enjoyable. The

really difficult part, as every author knows, comes with the writing.

Before giving so much as a thought to going to Pakistan or India, I read everything I could lay hands on to do with Kipling, and particularly with the writing of *Kim*. I worked my way through all the standard biographies, including Carrington, Birkenhead, Angus Wilson and the controversial Seymour-Smith, and the principal critical studies of his prose. I carefully re-read everything that he ever wrote about the Russian threat to India, notably his short story 'The Man Who Was', and his two poems, 'The Truce of the Bear' and 'The Ballad of the King's Jest'. I explored the library of the Kipling Society, now housed at the City University in London, and particularly the back-numbers of its journal, to see what had been said before. I also spent a day at Sussex University poring over the Kipling papers, in the hope of finding clues which might throw further light on *Kim*. I read the critical new introductions by leading Kipling scholars to three recent editions of the book. I studied, too, the detailed notes on *Kim* by Brigadier Alec Mason, late of the Indian Army, in *The Reader's Guide to Rudyard Kipling's Work*, and much else besides, including the views, at times surprisingly affectionate, of modern Indian writers and scholars.

One of my wisest moves was to shamelessly pick the brains of Mrs Lisa Lewis, whose knowledge of everything to do with Kipling and his works is both legendary and encyclopaedic, and who gave me a number of valuable leads in my quest. Among these was the whereabouts of the original manuscript of *Kim*, which contains significant textual changes made by the author. Armed with all this, I now felt confident enough to try to solve the first of the book's numerous riddles – *who* was Kim? Was he a total invention of Kipling's, or was there once a real-life Kim?

# Who Was Kim?

*H*E SAT, *in defiance of municipal orders, astride the gun Zam-Zammah on her brick platform opposite the old Ajaib-Gher – the Wonder House, as the natives call the Lahore Museum . . .*

In one of the best-remembered openings to any book, Kipling thus introduces us to his impish hero as he drums his bare heels against the great bronze cannon, repels other youthful invaders with well-directed kicks, and exchanges insults with the large, good-natured Punjabi policeman guarding the museum. To a passer-by, Kim looks much like any other Lahore thirteen-year-old, being 'burned as black as any native'. Yet although he knows every inch of every bazaar and alleyway in the old city, and is fluent in its numerous tongues, he is really a sahib, a European, 'a poor white of the very poorest'.

For Kim, Kipling tells us, is the orphan son of Kimball

O'Hara, an Irish colour-sergeant serving with his regiment in India, and Annie Shott, nursemaid to a British colonel's family. Both had died while Kim was very young – she first, of cholera, and he later, of alcohol and opium. Although supposedly looked after by his father's half-caste mistress, Kim has gone native. All his friends are Indian, whether Muslims, Hindus or Sikhs, and he comes and goes as he wishes from the second-hand furniture shop that his father's mistress runs by the square 'where the cheap cabs wait'. She smokes opium, and had indeed introduced Kim's father to the habit after he left the army and got a job as a railway foreman when his regiment returned home. If missionaries or members of charitable societies inquired about Kim, with well-intended concern over his moral welfare, she would insist that she was his mother's sister, and therefore his aunt, so preventing him from being taken away and placed in an orphanage.

When Kim's father died, he had left nothing but three documents, including Kim's birth-certificate and his own army discharge papers. The third document, written on parchment, was a somewhat mysterious one which he called his *ne varietur*, for those two words were written beneath his signature. These three documents, he would tell Kim in his opium hours, contained his destiny, and on no account was he ever to part with them. One day, he said, the colonel of the finest regiment in the world, riding on a horse at the head of 'nine hundred first-class devils, whose God was a Red Bull on a green field', would honour Kim. Then his father 'would weep bitterly in the broken rush chair on the veranda'. After O'Hara's death his mistress had sewn the three precious papers, which she could not herself understand, being illiterate, into a leather amulet-case which she hung around Kim's neck.

That is about as much as Kipling is prepared to tell us of Kim's background, and ever since people have wondered on whom, if anyone, he based his elusive character. Given that Kim is thirteen when the book opens, Kipling scholars have worked out from internal evidence – notably an earthquake and a frontier campaign he refers to – that the boy must have been born on May 1, 1865. That, significantly perhaps, was the year of Kipling's own birth, and there may therefore be more than a little of the author himself in this footloose European boy, with his love of freedom and horror of being caged. After all, had not Kipling tasted something of that carefree life during his own early, formative years in India? Born in Bombay, like most children of the Raj he was largely brought up by easygoing Indian servants, including an *ayah* and a bearer, who would take him into parts of the city not normally visited by Europeans, including temples closed to unbelievers and those of unsuitable caste.

Spending so much of his infancy with native servants meant that the young Rudyard was to become more fluent in Hindustani than in English, and it was perhaps this early linguistic intimacy with Indians that gave him his extraordinary facility for turning the vernacular of characters like Mahbub Ali, the Tibetan lama and Hurree Chunder Mookerjee into convincing English dialogue, surely one of *Kim*'s greatest joys. But it should not be forgotten, too, that in

writing *Kim* Kipling enjoyed the benefit of his father's profound knowledge of all things Indian – a contribution which
he acknowledges in his affectionate depiction of him as the
white-bearded curator of the Lahore 'Wonder House'. For,
as will be seen in due course, Lockwood Kipling, his gentle
and artistic father, was in fact the museum's founder and
first curator.

Given such a childhood, not to mention his own years in
Lahore on the *Civil and Military Gazette* and later on the
*Pioneer* in Allahabad, it is not perhaps surprising that a writer
of Kipling's imaginative genius should have created such a
character as the barefooted, freedom-loving Kim. But was
Kim a total invention, a throw-back to his own youthful
yearnings, the product of nostalgia for those idyllically happy
early days in Bombay – or was there a more solid basis to
him? Kipling himself gives us few clues, but this has not
deterred literary detectives from seeking a real-life model for
Kim. Apart from one rather vague tale, referred to without
source in a guidebook, of a barefoot European boy who used
to haunt the alleys of the old bazaar in Lahore, there are at
least two possible candidates. Both are strange stories in their
own right, which Kipling would very likely have come across,
either as a young journalist or as an insatiable reader.

The earliest of these was a mysterious young man named
Durie, the son of a British soldier and an Indian woman,
who in 1812 turned up in rags at the bungalow of a British
political officer, Mountstuart Elphinstone, after travelling
through Afghanistan disguised as a Muslim. 'His education',
Elphinstone recalled, 'must have been that of the lower order

of half-castes in India, and he spoke English ill.' Yet he brought back valuable intelligence on this land which the British had been unable to penetrate. Elphinstone, who himself had got no closer to Kabul than Peshawar during a Great Game mission four years earlier, made Durie write down everything that he could recall about his journey, which had included a residence of several months in both Kabul and Kandahar. This he published, as a twenty-page appendix, in his own book, *An Account of the Kingdom of Caboul.* Profoundly impressed by Durie, Elphinstone offered him a job, presumably to carry out similar undercover missions, at a salary of £150 a year. 'But though he was actually in a state of beggary,' Elphinstone tells us, 'he refused the offer.' Instead he set off for Bombay, there to embark on an Arab vessel bound for the Persian Gulf, from where he hoped to visit Baghdad. This was the last that Elphinstone ever saw or heard of this daring young adventurer.

An even stranger story, which Kipling certainly knew of, is that of Tim Doolan, the son of an Irish sergeant and a beautiful Tibetan girl. According to one version of this, the Irishman deserted from his regiment, stationed near Darjeeling, shortly after the Indian Mutiny of 1857, and fled with his lover across the Tibetan frontier, never to be heard of again. Then one day there appeared in the Darjeeling bazaar a strange youth with fair hair and blue eyes, but who spoke no English. Around his neck, however, was hung an amulet-case containing papers which showed him to be the son of the missing soldier. What became of him is not known, although one account maintains that he was hanged for murder. The story is said to have appeared in a Darjeeling newspaper called the *Pall Mall*, though Kipling scholars have been unable to find any trace of either the newspaper or the report, which was first cited by an Indian scholar writing in 1914, and subsequently by others. Unless the story is wholly apocryphal, and invented after *Kim*'s publication in 1901, the detail about the amulet-case containing Tim's (Kim's?) soldier-father's papers suggests that Kipling was aware of it when writing the book.

He unquestionably knew of another, rather different, version of this tale which appeared on August 8, 1889, five years before he started work on *Kim*, in *The Globe*, a London newspaper. Headlined AN EPISODE IN THE SIKKIM CAMPAIGN, this told how, following a battle with Tibetan invaders, a badly wounded Tibetan soldier with distinctly European features and complexion had been found on the battlefield. Questioned through an interpreter by the doctor treating him, the man said that his name was Namgay Doola, and that his father, Timlay Doola, was of the same colour as himself, while his mother was Tibetan. Both his parents were now dead.

Fascinated by the man's story, the doctor began to make further inquiries among the people of the region to see whether they knew anything more about Timlay Doola, and his origins. At first he drew a blank, but finally he tracked down an old lama who told him that many years earlier a big, red-headed European, wearing a red tunic and carrying a gun, had entered Sikkim from Darjeeling. He had settled down with a local woman there until the British entered

Sikkim in 1860, whereupon he fled to Tibet. Namgay, meanwhile, who had been befriended by the British doctor, sent
to his home in Tibet for some of his father's possessions.
Among these were a small brass crucifix, an old tobacco
stopper and – more significantly – a metal breastplate once
used by British soldiers to fasten their cross belts, this one
bearing a regimental number.

At the same time, a search of the records at Darjeeling
disclosed that a 'wild, harum-scarum' red-headed Irish soldier
named Tim Doolan, his health broken by drink and the
climate of the plains below, had deserted from a military
sanatorium in the hills and eloped with a young native
woman into Sikkim. A small search party had been sent after
Doolan, but he had fired on them and they had returned
without him. This was the last that had been seen of Doolan.
The doctor now had no doubt that Namgay Doola was the
son of Timlay Doola, otherwise Tim Doolan, deserter. When
Namgay's wounds had healed, he was set free, together with
the other Tibetan prisoners. Unlike them, however, he did
not return immediately to Tibet, but hung around the British
camp for some time, 'as if' – according to *The Globe* –
'reluctant to part from it'. In the end, taking with him small
gifts from his new British friends, he left, returning to his wife
and children in Tibet, never to be seen again by Europeans.

That Kipling was well aware of this strange tale is proved
by the publication, not long after *The Globe* article, of his
short story entitled simply 'Namgay Doola'. Although
the plot is pure fiction, the central figure is a mysterious
red-headed individual named Namgay Doola, whose

soldier-father was called Timlay Doola. Clearly half Irish, with a Tibetan mother, he has in his house a brass crucifix which once belonged to his father, whom he dimly remembers wearing a red tunic and whose musket and cap-badge he treasures. His own red-headed brood, moreover, can still sing the chorus, or something vaguely resembling it, of 'The Wearing of the Green', although they do not understand a word of it. They still worship Timlay Doola's Catholic deity, or rather something which could just pass for Him, and cross themselves before their grandfather's old brass crucifix.

Even if the precise character of Kim himself is not to be found in these real-life stories, it is fairly clear that Kipling obtained from at least one of them some of the inspiration and details for his narrative, just as he borrowed Namgay Doola and his soldier-father for his short story. Other characters in *Kim*, as will be seen in due course, are also borrowed from real life. Yet the overall idea for the book, or so Kipling scholars believe, sprang from an earlier novel which he abandoned, and finally destroyed, and whose contents are shrouded in considerable mystery, for no living person has ever read it.

Entitled *Mother Maturin*, after its principal character, the book explored – to quote its twenty-year-old author – 'the unutterable horrors of lower class Eurasian and native life'. It told the story of an Irishwoman who ran an opium den in Lahore, but who sent her daughter to school in England. The daughter returns, married to a British official, to live in Lahore, and very soon British Government secrets begin to be sold in the bazaar. Whether the young Kipling had any evidence of such impropriety will never be known, but certainly both his parents disliked the book. 'Mother says it's nasty but powerful,' wrote Kipling to his aunt, adding defensively: 'I *know* it to be in large measure true.'

Nonetheless, his father, whose opinion he greatly respected, urged him not to proceed with it, very likely because of its scandalous content and suggestion of leaked official secrets. After all, he and his wife, prominent members of the small European community, had to live in Lahore, where the publication of such a book would, to put it mildly, cause a sensation. In the event, Kipling accepted his father's advice, and the work advanced no further than page 237. But it was not all wasted, for Kipling was later able to salvage some of its less scandalous parts and incorporate these into *Kim*. For this reason, his biographer Angus Wilson argues, we should be grateful to Lockwood Kipling, for the final work is Kipling's 'masterpiece . . . far more than any simple connecting of opium dens with Government House, the Club and the Mall'.

As for the character of Kim, however, all that Kipling is prepared to tell us is that the idea came to him in the summer of 1892, before being shelved for a while. 'I had a vague notion', he wrote years later in *Something of Myself*, 'of an Irish boy, born in India and mixed up with native life. I went as far as to make him the son of a private in an Irish battalion, and christened him "Kim of the 'Rishti" – short, that is, for Irish.' Indeed, *Kim o' the 'Rishti* is the title at the top of his original manuscript. Today this is to be found in the British Library, and it was there that my journey into the world of Kim really began.

\*

Written in a tiny, spidery hand, with frequent crossings-out and other alterations, the original draft of *Kim* is a compositor's nightmare. Notes in the margin, however, suggest that some chapters may have been given to a secretary to be typed before going to the printer for setting. There are no signs of an editor having worked on the manuscript, all the alterations being in Kipling's own hand. Today carefully preserved in a handsome leather-bound volume, British Library manuscript no. 44840 was presented to the nation in October 1925, eleven years before his death, by Kipling himself. His sole proviso was that it must not be reproduced photographically, which means that I can only describe it.

I suppose I had half hoped to discover, perhaps lurking somewhere in the margins, some new clue to Kim's origins. Any such expectations, though, were soon dashed. Apart from a few doodles, including a neat pen-and-ink sketch of a Buddhist prayer-wheel, the manuscript yielded no such secrets. Nonetheless, the numerous crossings-out and substituted words and phrases give an interesting insight into how Kipling enhanced his narrative. Among several such changes of mind on the book's opening page, for example, his description of Kim being 'burned black as any native' first appears as 'looked like a half caste'. Other second thoughts must have occurred to Kipling at a later stage, for there are, in places, noticeable differences between the so-called 'original draft' in the British Library and the first English edition of *Kim*. But these, on the whole, are of no great consequence, except perhaps to Kipling scholars, and I shall only refer to them when they throw light on our narrative.

The story of Kim did not, in fact, first appear in book form, but rather as a magazine serial in America. For it was initially published, between December 1900 and October 1901, in *McClure's Magazine*, a New York monthly, in which a number of Kipling's short stories had already appeared. In January 1901, serialisation of *Kim* began in the British magazine *Cassell's*. Finally, on October 1, 1901, the first edition of the book appeared, published at six shillings by Macmillan, with illustrations by Kipling's highly gifted artist father. The latter are extremely important, for while readers of *Kim* will have their own conception of what the various characters looked like, Lockwood Kipling's sensitive portraits of Kim, the old lama, Mahbub Ali and Hurree Chunder Mookerjee presumably approximate most closely to Kipling's own perception of them, or even to the real-life individuals on whom they were wholly or partly based. It is a pity, therefore, that these portraits, originally executed as bas-reliefs, were not used in subsequent editions of *Kim*.

The first English edition of 1901 was closely followed, two weeks later, by the first American one. Ever since, there has been a succession of editions and translations – including the French one which stopped the German sniper's bullet. But just how many copies of *Kim* have been sold over the years it is impossible to discover, despite approaches to Macmillan's and to Kipling's agents, for no record appears to have been kept. However, overall sales must easily have topped the million mark. Like all Kipling's works, *Kim* went out of copyright in 1987, fifty years after his death, entitling anyone to bring out a new edition. That year both Penguin Books and Oxford University Press reissued it in paperback, with other publishers following suit. Recently, however, new European Union legislation has extended copyright from fifty years after an author's death to seventy, abruptly ending this publishers' bonanza. The principal beneficiary in Kipling's case will be the National Trust, which owns his copyright, as well as Bateman's, his former Sussex home.

\*

I now felt that I had discovered as much as I was ever likely to about Kim's origins from literary and other sources. It would seem that Kipling's idea for such a character derived, both consciously and unconsciously, from real-life tales of

Kim-like individuals to which he added elements borrowed from his own Bombay childhood and his own intimate knowledge of Indian low-life. There are also faint but recognisable similarities between Kim and Mowgli, the Indian wolf-boy in *The Jungle Book*, first published in 1894, when Kipling was beginning to work on *Kim*. However, unless some previously unknown correspondence or other evidence comes unexpectedly to light, the precise genesis of Kim can never be anything more than speculation.

But before we catch the plane for Lahore to try to discover what, if anything, still survives of Kim's world, one further task awaits us. As even those who have not yet read *Kim* must by now be aware, it takes place against the heady background of the Great Game, the century-long Anglo-Russian struggle for the mastery of Asia which, to the British at least, ultimately meant India. We must therefore consider for a moment the political and historical context of Kipling's narrative of this youngster who is talent-spotted for the Great Game.

It has been pointed out, more than once, that by the time Kipling wrote *Kim* the Great Game was virtually over, for British and Tsarist differences were finally settled in 1907 under the Anglo-Russian Convention, an accord generally accepted as marking the end of this shadowy contest. That is easily seen with hindsight, but in the mid-1890s, when Kipling first embarked on *Kim*, the Great Game was still very far from over. Colonel Francis Younghusband's expedition to Lhasa, to investigate rumours of a Russian presence in the Tibetan capital, and generally regarded as the last major move in the Great Game, was still some years off. And that, moreover, is assuming that the events described in *Kim* were intended by Kipling to be contemporaneous with its publication. Indeed, as we have already seen, Kim was supposedly born in the same year as Kipling himself, 1865. Add thirteen, for that was his age when the book opens, and it brings us only to 1878, when the Great Game was at its height. The book spans four years, until Kim is rising seventeen, a time when there was no let-up in the imperial struggle and the perceived threat to British India from 'the great deliverer from the North'.

But it was not only fear of Russian armies pouring down from Central Asia into India which caused Raj strategists to lose sleep. There was also the Enemy Within. Many Europeans still remembered the appalling horrors of the Indian Mutiny, only twenty years earlier. Their ultimate nightmare was that a Russian advance towards India's frontiers would trigger off a second Mutiny, with native regiments going over wholesale to the enemy and their agents within the country. Indeed, there were frequent scares about Tsarist *agents provocateurs* at work. At the same time many had doubts about the loyalty of some Indian Army units and certain Indian princes, many of whom had their own well-equipped private armies. The latter were said to total twice the combined strength of the British and sepoy troops in India. The *Pioneer*, the newspaper for which Kipling was later to work, was notoriously Russophobic, perpetually demanding that more British troops and artillery be sent to India. In the light of all this, one can readily understand why Colonel Creighton and his trusted agents, such as Mahbub Ali and Hurree Chunder Mookerjee, maintained their unsleeping watch for treachery both within and beyond India's frontiers. Indeed, it was this ultimate Raj nightmare of a joint conspiracy between an enemy without and an enemy within which, as we shall see in due course, gave Kipling his plot involving 'five confederated Kings, a sympathetic Northern Power, a Hindu banker in Peshawur, a firm of gun-makers in Belgium, and an important, semi-independent Mohammedan ruler to the south'.

Long before he wrote *Kim*, or even came to work in India, Kipling himself had begun to show signs of Russophobia. As a teenager at boarding school in England he had proposed a motion in a school debate in which he argued that 'the advance of the Russians in Central Asia is hostile to the British Power'. His Russian-speaking headmaster, a gentle, liberal-minded intellectual, had opposed the motion in person, but to no avail, it being carried by 21 votes to 9. However, most of the boys were the sons of Raj officials or Indian Army officers, and thus greatly influenced by the prevailing attitudes of that class. This, moreover, was in 1882, shortly after the Russians had smashed Turcoman resistance at Geok-Tepe, their great desert fortress, opening the way for the building of a strategic railway eastwards towards Afghanistan and ultimately – or so the British feared – India. Indeed at one time, Kipling had seriously considered taking Russian lessons from his headmaster, a man he greatly revered. A highly unusual step for a schoolboy in those days, it had in the end come to nothing.

## Who Was Kim?

While working in Lahore on the *Civil and Military Gazette*
Kipling's duties had included translating reports of Russian
activities in Central Asia from a French-language newspaper
published in Moscow and another received regularly from
St Petersburg. The *Gazette*'s own readership consisted almost

entirely of Indian Army officers and government servants,
many of whom Kipling met socially at the Punjab Club,
who expected to be kept fully informed of Tsarist machina-
tions which threatened India. In the spring of 1885, when he
was still only nineteen, he was sent as his paper's special
correspondent to Peshawar, on the North-West Frontier. For
the Viceroy, Lord Dufferin, was due to hold talks with the
Emir of Afghanistan, Abdur Rahman, aimed at securing his
support, if it became necessary, against the Russians. The
Emir's arrival at the frontier was much delayed, and Kipling
had to find material for thirteen articles, totalling 30,000
words, while he waited at the mouth of the Khyber Pass.
This episode, together with his regular monitoring of the

Russian press, must have given the young Kipling a very thorough early grounding in Great Game skulduggery. Indeed, it was not long before he began to introduce Russophobic themes into his short stories and even his poems. Two obvious examples are 'The Man Who Was' – a chilling tale of a Russian officer's visit to a British regiment in Peshawar – and 'The Truce of the Bear' – an equally chilling poem about a bear which is not to be trusted.

Finally, returning to *Kim*, it should be remembered that this was written at a time when the focus of the Great Game had begun to move eastwards from Afghanistan towards Tibet. It was no secret in India or in Whitehall that the Russians were interested in Tibet, for the famous Tsarist explorer Colonel Nikolai Prejevalsky had made two unsuccessful attempts, together with an armed Cossack escort, to reach the holy city of Lhasa. When Lord Curzon, a lifelong Russophobe, was appointed Viceroy of India in January 1899, he brought with him from London almost paranoid suspicions of Tsarist ambitions in the region. Very soon these suspicions began to settle on Tibet, over which, Curzon became more and more convinced, the Russians had signed a secret and treacherous treaty with the Chinese. It was these fears which would eventually lead to his dispatch of an armed expedition to Lhasa to try to find out what precisely was going on there. This growing official interest in Tibet, then still a forbidden and mysterious land, perhaps explains why Kipling chose to make it bulk so large in *Kim*. For he could, just as easily, have made the lama a Muslim holy man from Afghanistan or Central Asia, rather than from Tibet, on a similar religious quest.

All that, however, is more than enough about the historical setting of *Kim*: it is high time that we set out in pursuit of Kim himself, on a journey which will carry us back nearly one hundred years in time, to a world that no longer exists except in the now dim memories of a few old men and women, both British and Indian, who once served the Raj. And very soon, as the obituary columns show with increasing frequency, the last of these will have departed – perhaps to join Kim and the lama, Colonel Creighton and Lurgan Sahib, Mahbub Ali and Hurree Chunder Mookerjee, in the Valhalla of the Great Game, or wherever else they may be.

Not long after my visit to the British Library, I left Heathrow airport for Lahore, with my old and heavily annotated copy of *Kim* in my pocket. If I achieved nothing else, at least I would do something I had yearned to do for as long as I could remember. And that was to re-read, perhaps for the hundredth time, the book which had helped to mould my life, but this time in the land which had given it birth. Rarely, in a lifetime of travel, have I felt so exhilarated.

# 2

# *Enter the Lama*

I BEGAN, I must confess, to re-read *Kim* on the eight-hour flight out. It would have been too much to ask that I wait until I reached Lahore. But it also gave me the opportunity to mull over something that had been worrying me ever since I decided to explore the world of *Kim*. If I was to write a book about it, should I assume that everyone had read Kipling's masterpiece, since they would not be reading this if they had not? Or should I assume that no one had read it, and that even if they had it was probably in childhood and they would largely have forgotten it? I finally decided to sketch in the story, working it into my own narrative episode by episode as I followed in Kim's footsteps.

Shorn of all its magic – its innocence, its compassion, its humour and its extraordinary sense of freedom – the story of Kim's recruitment into the secret service can be told quite simply. It need hardly be said, however, that there is absolutely no substitute for reading *Kim* itself. For not only is it a deeply enjoyable book, but also a profoundly uplifting one, especially for anyone whose spirits are at a low ebb. It emits an intense luminescence, like that spilling out of a landscape by Turner. A friend of mine suffering from a nasty bout of depression swore that reading *Kim* totally cured him. Indeed, some scholars believe that Kipling, who suffered badly from melancholia, wrote *Kim* to cure his own depression.

Kim, as we already know, is white, which perhaps makes it easier for the European to identify with him. He is the thirteen-year-old orphan son of a colour-sergeant and a nurse-maid, both Irish. Supposedly looked after by his late father's mistress, he is left free to roam wherever he wishes, for she, like his father, is an opium addict. His friends are the boys of Lahore's native quarter, rather than the children of the city's European families. He has, in other words, 'gone native', adopting the dress, language and habits of his Muslim and Hindu friends, slipping easily from one to the other, or back to the ragged poor white that he really is. One set of spare clothes, those of a low-caste Hindu urchin, he keeps in a secret cache in a timber yard near the Punjab High Court.

Quick-witted, and wise beyond his years, he is acutely aware of all that goes on in the teeming streets and bazaars of Lahore. With a gift for tart repartee and flattery in several languages, not to mention an aptitude for lying, Kim is well known in the old city, where he has earned himself the nickname 'Little Friend of all the World'. He lives largely by begging and by carrying out discreet missions, usually at night, for a strange assortment of patrons, for he prides himself on knowing every alleyway, short-cut and rooftop in Lahore. It is of course this elusiveness, this ability to melt into the background, which Kipling has bestowed upon Kim, that very soon brings him to the attention of Colonel Creighton, the Raj spymaster.

As all who have read *Kim* well know, the story opens as Kim and his friends are playing on the ancient gun Zam-Zammah, outside the Lahore museum. Suddenly, from the direction of the nearby bazaar, there appears a strange figure – 'such a man as Kim, who thought he knew all castes, had never seen'. His face was yellow and wrinkled 'like that of Fook Shing, the Chinese bootmaker in the bazaar', while on his head he wore 'a gigantic sort of tam-o'-shanter'. His clothing consisted of 'fold upon fold of dingy stuff like horse-blanketing', while from his belt hung a long open-work iron pencase 'and a wooden rosary such as holy men wear'. His eyes, Kim noticed, 'turned up at the corners and looked like little slits of onyx'.

The newcomer shuffled over to where the boys were playing. 'O Children,' he asked in Urdu, pointing to the museum, 'what is that big house?' Kim, who was riveted by this extraordinary figure, answered that it was the Ajaib-Gher, 'the Wonder House'. Then he began to shower him with questions, asking him who he was, where he had come from, and what had brought him to Lahore. The old man replied that he was a lama, or holy man, from far-off Tibet, 'where the air and water are fresh and cool'. He had come to India to find the Buddhist holy places 'before I die', and to Lahore because he believed that in the 'Wonder House' there were many sacred sculptures and other holy relics.

Ever seeking excitement, Kim led the old lama through the museum turnstile into the entrance hall. Here were displayed several large sculptures and reliefs removed from crumbling stupas in the far north of India. The lama was overwhelmed at the sight of these treasures. 'The Lord! The Lord! It is Sakya Muni himself,' he half sobbed in front of one relief. Then suddenly, attracted perhaps by the commotion, there appeared the white-bearded European curator. Kim slipped quickly away, leaving the two men together.

The curator, a kindly, courteous man, then invited the Tibetan into his office, where they spoke excitedly about many things. But these meant little to Kim who, the moment the door was shut, lay down before it with his ear pressed to a crack so as not to miss a word. Eventually the two men parted, though not before the curator had given his visitor his own spare reading glasses to replace the lama's badly scratched and primitive pair. In return the grateful old man had presented the Englishman with his antique Tibetan pen-case, declaring: 'It is something old, even as I am.' He promised to return on his way home to Tibet after completing his pilgrimage, the main purpose of which was to find the sacred river, where Buddha's arrow fell, and which washes away the sins of all who bathe in it. All that he knew was that it lay somewhere in India, a land of very many rivers.

Such then is the opening scene of *Kim*, with the introduction of the book's two leading characters – 'two wonderfully attractive men', Edward Said calls them. Some critics have even argued that the saintly old Tibetan lama, so sympathetically portrayed by Kipling, is the real hero of the book, gently pushing Kim into second place. Certainly Kipling makes it very difficult for the reader not to be drawn to this vulnerable old man, so unworldly and pure of heart, who succeeds in making goodness seem positively attractive. In less skilled hands he might have come across as sanctimonious or self-righteous. All this brings us to the intriguing question of who, if anyone, the lama is based on.

Kipling himself does not tell us, although he offers us

some clues in *Kim*. The old man is described by another character as a 'Red Lama', and in his conversation with the museum curator, he reveals that he has come, via Kulu, from the Tibetan lamasery of 'Such-zen, opposite the Painted Rocks, four months' march away'. Certainly the curator knew where that was, for he astonished his visitor by producing an album of photographs showing 'that very place, perched on its crag, overlooking the gigantic valley of many-hued strata'. The name 'Such-zen' meant nothing to me, however, and I could find no trace of it in Sir Charles Bell's four great works on the people, religion and history of Tibet, or anything remotely resembling it.

My only remaining hope of discovering whether Kipling had invented this lamasery, together with the lama, was to consult a Tibetan expert. Luckily, having once written a book about the Western penetration of Tibet, *Trespassers on the Roof of the World*, I knew a number of leading authorities on the country. It was obviously unfair to trouble them all on such a comparatively unimportant and imprecise matter, so I settled for someone who I hoped might suffer fools more gladly, and who I also knew loved *Kim*. This was Zara Fleming, a Tibetan-speaking scholar, formerly with the Victoria and Albert Museum, and an old friend, who has travelled widely in Tibet and is in close and regular contact with Tibetans, both inside and outside the country. I sent her a copy of *Kim* – for a friend had gone off with hers and not returned it – and asked her if she could possibly identify the lama as being based on a real individual who had once made a pilgrimage to India.

The sole clues were the name of his (very likely fictitious) monastery, the fact that he had a friend who was Abbot of the 'Lung-Cho' monastery, and finally – revealed further into the narrative – that the old man styled himself 'Teshoo Lama'. Zara entered into the spirit of the quest, and carefully studied the clues, before phoning to say that she had been forced to admit defeat. She pointed out that 'Teshoo Lama' simply meant 'Learned One', and could apply to many Tibetan clergy, and she knew of no celebrated pilgrim who had travelled to India from Tibet at around this time. So far as the two monasteries were concerned, however, 'Such-zen' could be a corruption by Kipling, who spoke no Tibetan, of 'Tso-chen', a 'Red Hat' monastery. Similarly, 'Lung-Cho' monastery could be 'Lung-Kar', a remote and little-known lamasery.

This seemed a bit nebulous and I was about to conclude that the lama was the one principal character who had been totally made up by Kipling. But then I received a letter from another friend, Annabel Walker, who was at that moment researching her life of Sir Aurel Stein, the great Central Asian explorer and archaeologist, about whom I had once written in *Foreign Devils on the Silk Road*. Astonishingly, among Stein's voluminous papers in the Bodleian, she had come upon a vital clue. It was contained in a letter to Stein from his old friend Lockwood Kipling, who was almost certainly the model for the kindly, white-bearded Englishman who had so warmly received the lama. Writing on May 16, 1902, eight years after his retirement from the Lahore museum, he enquired: 'I wonder whether you have seen my son's "Kim", and recognised an old Lama whom you saw at the old Museum and at the School.'

Thanks to Annabel, I had now established that Kipling had a real flesh-and-blood Tibetan lama in mind when he portrayed him in such detail in *Kim*. Also, thanks to Zara, we know that he may even have come from an actual monastery. Tso-chen, she informs me, lies in a remote and rarely visited part of Tibet, 450 miles east of Simla and 200 miles north of Kathmandu. Alas, she believes it to be one of many Tibetan monasteries to have suffered badly at the hands of the Chinese Red Guards.

Two further pieces of evidence which tend to bear all this out were also supplied to me by Zara Fleming. First, Tso-chen lamasery is a Red Hat monastery, and our lama, Kipling tells us, belonged to that sect rather than to the Yellow Hat sect. Yet, Zara informs me, the Yellow Hats were far better known in India in Kipling's day than the Red Hats, who were little known, if at all. Hence, had Kipling simply invented his lama, he would more likely have made him a Yellow Hat. Just to clinch things, Zara points out that the Lung-Kar monastery, where the lama's friend is the Abbot, is the nearest one, out of hundreds scattered across Tibet, to his own, which seems more than a mere coincidence.

*

On the night I flew into Lahore, impatient to immerse myself in the story without delay, I hurried down the crowded Mall, the city's main thoroughfare, towards where I knew lay the museum. Very soon, in the far distance, I spotted what I was looking for. Through the honking, swirling traffic I could just discern the unmistakable silhouette of 'Kim's gun', as Zam-Zammah has come to be called. And there, clambering over it in the gloaming, pushing and pulling one another, were several young Pakistani boys. Very little, I was heartened to see, had changed in the last hundred years or so.

To try to prevent these would-be Kims from playing on Lahore's most famous relic, recently renovated at considerable expense, the authorities had built a concrete moat around the plinth on which the ancient gun stands. This they had judged to be far too wide for anyone to leap across, though just to make sure they had surrounded it with a low iron railing topped with shin-high spikes. But they had greatly underestimated the agility of these young urchins who were busily springing back and forth across both these lines of defence.

As I watched, a large traffic policeman – he could easily have been the big Punjabi constable in *Kim* – fought his way through the riot of taxis and motor-bikes, bullock-carts and bicycles, and sternly ordered the boys off the gun. Three minutes later, however, when he was safely out of sight, they were back again astride Zam-Zammah – once the terror of northern India, but now, just as it was in Kipling's day, an adventure playground for young Kims. One thing did sadden me, though. None of these boys were aware that they were re-enacting English literature in their antics on the ancient Zam-Zammah. Indeed, so totally forgotten is Kipling's story in Lahore today that most people there think that Kim is the name of the gun, and not that of the small boy who once sat astride it 'in defiance of municipal orders'.

Before earning its honourable retirement on its plinth opposite the Lahore museum, Zam-Zammah had distinguished itself in numerous campaigns, and had changed

hands more than once, during a stormy career of some sixty years. In addition to its awesome size and firepower, this 'taker of the Ramparts of Heaven' – to quote a Persian inscription on its barrel – was widely held to possess divine powers, and served as a powerful talisman for victory. It was, in its day, the largest gun ever made in India, being over fourteen feet long, with a calibre of ten inches. Cast in Lahore in 1762, on the orders of Ahmad Shah Durrani, the Afghan warrior-king in whose domains the Punjab then lay, it once had a twin. However this was lost during a river crossing while being dragged back to Kabul by Ahmad Shah's victorious artillerymen, and today it lies somewhere at the bottom of the Chenab river, forty miles west of Lahore.

Zam-Zammah's last battle was in 1818, when it sustained terminal damage. Thereafter it was displayed, in veneration, at the city's Delhi Gate, where it remained until 1870. After one further move, the significance of which I shall explain shortly, it finally came to rest where it now stands. Today Kipling, not to mention Kim, might be hard-pressed to recognise the green-bronze 'fire-breathing dragon' that once stood guard over the 'Wonder House'. For its great barrel is now a gleaming gold, the result of its recent restoration. But a few more years of exposure to Lahore's corrosive traffic fumes will, no doubt, take the shine off it.

Such then is the story of Zam-Zammah, immortalised by Kipling in *Kim*, and perhaps the most famous gun in the world, certainly to those of my generation. But that, of course, is not all that this spot has to offer those who arrive here, *Kim* in hand. Just across the road from Zam-Zammah, either side of which flows the Mall traffic, stands the 'Wonder House' itself, a fine example of what Jan Morris has described as the Anglo-Mogul school of architecture. Over the years, successive generations of Kipling scholars and *Kim* pilgrims have stood in its ornate entrance hall and tried to envisage that celebrated meeting between East and West, between the old Tibetan lama and the white-haired English curator, and to work out where it was that Kim eavesdropped on their conversation through a crack in the door.

For everyone knows that Kipling's father was curator of the 'Wonder House' and that Kipling himself knew every inch of it, being very close to his father, whose contribution to *Kim* he gratefully acknowledged. In fact, in addition to working as a reporter on the *Civil and Military Gazette*, he sometimes gave his father a hand in the museum, and it is not impossible that he, too, was present when the old lama visited it. Indeed, I have often heard people say that little has really changed in the museum since Kipling described it so lovingly in *Kim*. I have to confess that, apart from the disappearance of the 'self-registering turnstile' which Kim and the lama passed through, I thought much the same, following an earlier visit some years before.

It was only when I read Lockwood Kipling's remark, in his letter to Aurel Stein of 1902, about the lama they had seen together 'at the *old* Museum' (my italics) that I began to wonder what he meant. Had there perhaps been an earlier museum? It did not take me long to establish that the present museum was completed in 1894. Kipling's father could hardly be referring to this, only eight years later, as the 'old' museum. There must, therefore, have been a previous one, of which he had been the curator. If so, this one, and not today's museum, is the one described in *Kim*. To clinch it, I discovered that Lockwood Kipling left India for home in 1893, following his retirement, a whole year before the new museum opened. But more significantly, Rudyard himself left India for good in 1889, *five* years before it opened. He therefore could never even have set eyes on it, let alone have described it as vividly as he does in *Kim*.

All that remained now was for me to discover what I could about the 'old' museum – the real 'Wonder House' of *Kim*'s opening pages. I borrowed from my publishers a copy of their celebrated *Murray's Handbook of the Punjab*, published in 1883 and now extremely rare, and there I found the answer. There was indeed an earlier museum which was, according to the guidebook, 'called by the Indians Aja'ib Ghar'. It stood next to the Central Post Office, only a stone's throw from the present museum, and was housed in a building originally constructed for the great Punjab Exhibition of 1864. This was to have been replaced by a new and more suitable building, the guidebook tells us, adding: 'but funds have not been forthcoming'. It went on to list some of the museum's treasures, including the ancient Graeco-Buddhist masterpieces described so memorably in *Kim*, at the sight of which the lama was moved almost to tears. Finally I came upon the statement that confirmed everything – 'On a raised platform in front of the entrance is the famous gun called the Zamzamah', the guidebook declared.

Eventually, following a public appeal to commemorate Queen Victoria's Golden Jubilee, the necessary money for the new museum was raised. In 1890 work began on the building, the design of which was largely based on Lockwood Kipling's concepts, although he left India before it was completed. Next, the entire contents of the old museum were moved into the new galleries, of which there were originally only six, though this has grown over the years to twenty-three. Today it is the second largest museum on the subcontinent after Calcutta, and is famous for its Buddhist and Islamic collections. It receives some 600,000 visitors a year, though only a small percentage of these are from the West. Some of the latter, however, arrive clutching their copies of *Kim*, convinced that they are entering the 'Wonder House'. Even Rudyard Kipling's biographer, Charles Carrington, got it wrong, declaring: 'The Museum stands, just as it is described in the first chapter of *Kim* . . .' Angus Wilson, in his biography, falls into the same trap. 'Here', he writes, 'stands the Museum where for nearly twenty years Lockwood Kipling was curator.'

In actual fact, the real 'Wonder House' *does*, at the time of writing, still stand, although it has come down in the world since Kim's day. No longer a museum filled with Buddhist art treasures, it has been turned into a covered market, selling a host of everyday goods. It is to be found several hundred yards to the left of the Lahore museum, on the same side of the Mall, but across another, secondary road. Of course, nobody – least of all myself – wishes to see their fond illusions demolished. It might have been better, on second thoughts, to have kept quiet, leaving the myth of the 'Wonder House' intact. But whatever the truth, the Lahore museum today is a treasure-house of Asian art, with a remarkable atmosphere of its own. And among those treasures the discerning visitor will recognise the great Graeco-Buddhist sculptures – 'done, savants know how long since, by forgotten workmen whose hands were feeling . . . for the mysteriously transmitted Grecian touch' – so exquisitely described in *Kim*.

I asked the curator whether pilgrims still travelled from Tibet to see these sacred Buddhist treasures. 'Very few,' he thought. Far more, however, come from Japan, China, Sri Lanka and other countries with Buddhist traditions, often in groups. One such party of Buddhists from a Japanese university arrived to find the museum closed for cleaning. 'They started to weep,' he told me, 'explaining that they were being denied access to their shrine.' The museum staff were so moved by their plight that they allowed them in, 'whereupon they fell on the ground, weeping with joy, before the sacred sculptures'.

The lama in *Kim*, like these twentieth-century pilgrims, was part of a very ancient tradition which brought Buddhist monks enormous distances, originally on foot, to see the holy places of their faith in India, the land of its birth. Among the very earliest of these were converts from China, which the revolutionary new religion had reached via the Karakorum and Pamir passes. The most celebrated such pilgrim was the intrepid traveller Fa-hsien, who in AD 399 set out westwards along the ancient Silk Road to Kashgar, before turning southwards into India. There he first visited the Buddhist kingdom of Gandhara, lying in the Peshawar valley region of what is now north-western Pakistan. It was here that centuries later British-Indian archaeologists discovered many of the Graeco-Buddhist sculptures which so astonished the lama in the 'Wonder House'. For these were the first representations of the Buddha in human form, he having always before been depicted by a mystical symbol such as a single footprint, a wheel, a stupa or a tree. This explains the old lama's cry of 'The Lord! The Lord! It is Sakya Muni himself', when he found himself face to face with these epoch-making sculptures for the first time.

But in exploring the mystery of the lama's origins and the truth about the 'Wonder House' we have digressed long enough. We must pick up the threads of the story again where we left it earlier in the chapter – as the lama is leaving the museum to begin his quest for the River of the Arrow, 'which washes away all taint and speckle of sin'. His task has been made all the harder for him by the loss, through fever, of his young *chela*, or disciple, who had begged for him on their four-month journey from Tibet, and for whom the old man still pines. Feeling bewildered, lonely and hungry, he wanders over towards Zam-Zammah, where he sits down exhausted in the shade. But the next moment the big Punjabi constable on duty outside the museum bellows at him: 'Do not sit under that gun.'

Happily, though, help is at hand in the impudent person of Kim, who has followed him out of the museum 'like a shadow'. Silencing the policeman (in a voice loud enough for all to hear) with an accusation as embarrassing as it was untrue, Kim told the lama to ignore the order and remain seated where he was. Then, as the unfortunate constable shuffled off, knowing that Kim's shrill voice 'could call up legions of bad bazaar boys', Kim squatted down beside the old man and began gently to question him. For what he had overheard through the crack in the curator's door had greatly excited him with its promise of mysterious things. 'The lama was his trove,' wrote Kipling in *Kim*, 'and he proposed to take possession.' A more politically correct explanation of the thirteen-year-old urchin's actions has been offered by an American academic, who informs us, apparently in all seriousness, that Kim, 'with the insight and intuition of the born colonialist, recognises that the lama is a new territory worth annexing'.

But whichever point of view you subscribe to, that moment was to mark the beginning of a strange and touching friendship, between youth and old age, which would lead, in the quest for the sacred river, to the altogether murkier waters of the Great Game.

# 3

# *Enter Mahbub Ali*

IT WOULD BE tempting, when retelling the story of
*Kim*, to borrow heavily from the original, quoting in
Kipling's own words its most memorable scenes and descriptions. So full, in fact, is it of unforgettable passages that the
problem would be to know where to stop. By means of such
plunder it would not be difficult to enlist Kipling's literary
wizardry to bejewel one's own pedestrian efforts. But I have
tried, at all costs, to resist any such temptation to break the
Tenth Commandment, having no wish to produce a sort of
ersatz, plagiarised version of *Kim*. My aim, born of a strong
missionary zeal, is to persuade people to rediscover Kipling's
Indian masterpiece, but in its entirety, not in some abridged
form. By throwing fresh light on the story – especially the
role of the Great Game in it, and the blowing of the covers
of some of Kipling's 'cast' – I hope to make their rediscovery
more rewarding. For quite apart from the sheer joy of

travelling with Kim and the lama across 'the fair land of Hind', the more one delves into this great spy story the more one enjoys the subtleties and secrets hidden within its pages.

Although I have used direct quotations from *Kim* where my own words alone would be painfully inadequate, I have done so as sparingly as possible. For the most part I have simply compressed the story, and then only to the minimum required to make my own narrative comprehensible. Some of the book's finest passages have been cut to the bone, while others will not be found here at all. An immediate example of this is Kim's expedition to the bazaar with the hungry lama's begging bowl, with which he returns, the bowl heaped with steaming vegetable curry and rice. In *Kim* his comical encounter with the woman shopkeeper, not to mention the sacred Brahmini bull, fills two pages, which should not on any account be missed. But to proceed with our narrative. While the lama sleeps off his meal beneath Zam-Zammah, Kim changes into his Hindu urchin's garb. Then, to the old man's utter confusion, he returns in his new guise.

We now come to a crucial moment in the story, as Kim makes the decision which dominates the rest of the book. Failing to recognise Kim as the ragged street-child who took him into the 'Wonder House' and begged for him when he was hungry, the bewildered Tibetan asks him: 'Who are you?' To this Kim replies softly: 'Thy *chela*.' Then, sitting back on his heels, he adds: 'I have never seen any one like to thee in all this my life. I go with thee to Benares.' With these words was forged one of the most original and sensitively portrayed friendships in English literature – between the saintly Tibetan pilgrim and the elusive, chameleon-like white youth, already a man of the world at thirteen, who, Kipling tells us, 'had known all evil since he could speak', and 'was hand in glove with men who had led lives stranger than anything Haroun al Raschid dreamed of'.

This relationship between such opposites has been compared by Angus Wilson to that of Don Quixote and Sancho Panza, while others have likened it to that of Mr Pickwick and Sam Weller. For, like *Kim*, both these other classics revolve around an innocent master and a streetwise disciple. And all three minders, in their different ways, protect their masters from the consequences of their unworldliness. Yet, as Philip Mason points out in his study of Kipling, there are very marked differences between them. Whereas, in the last resort, Sam Weller uses his fists, 'Kim wins hearts with his tongue', though Mason forgets that Kim, too, resorts to his fists – not to mention banging his enemy's head against a boulder – while protecting the lama, though that is still a long way off in the story.

But regardless of the literary antecedents of this unlikely pair, it was my good fortune, with *Kim* in hand, to enjoy their company during their numerous adventures. My first move was to take a taxi (Kim and the lama took a horse-drawn tram, but these no longer exist) from the affluent end of Lahore, with its great Mogul mosques, palaces and tombs, to where the fortress-like railway station stands, surrounded by sleazy hotels, just as it did in Kim's day. For it was here in the Kashmir Serai, which today has all but vanished, that

Kim had a friend among the horse-dealers who he felt sure would let them sleep on his floor.

Kipling knew the native quarters of old Lahore better than any other Englishman. For on most summer nights, after he had seen the midnight edition of the *Civil and Military Gazette* to press, he would wander the darkened streets, with their opium dens and brothels, trying to escape the oppressive heat, and only returning home at dawn. It was a Lahore he loved to write about, and it was this intimacy with the old city – much of it burned down in 1947 during the dreadful holocaust which followed India's partition – that inspired some of his most powerful writing. Best known, perhaps, is 'The City of Dreadful Night', a haunting description of death and sleeplessness in Lahore. But it is also found in the early pages of *Kim*, where Kipling paints a brilliant picture of the lama and Kim's arrival at the Kashmir Serai, 'that huge open square over against the railway station, surrounded with arched cloisters, where the camel and horse caravans put up on their return from Central Asia'.

Today it is where the long-distance buses put in, and where young back-packers prefer to stay, for there are plenty of cheap hotels in this raffish part of town. One favourite guidebook of young travellers warns, however, that they 'should take extreme care in this area', which has long enjoyed an evil reputation. 'Hotel staff', cautions the Lonely Planet Guide, 'are incredibly talented at distracting even the most switched-on visitors and separating them from their money belts. Some of the tricks used include spiked tea, soft drinks or cigarettes; early morning requests for passport information;

two or more staff in the room at the same time; trick doors or windows through which to enter your room when you're out.' It adds: 'If you insist on staying in this area, check windows, doors and ceilings for possible ways of breaking in.' Despite such warnings, the publishers note, 'we continue to get letters from people who've been ripped off'.

In Kipling's day it was just as raffish, but it was also a lot more colourful. 'Here', Kipling writes in *Kim*, 'were all manner of Northern folk, tending tethered ponies and kneeling camels; loading and unloading bales and bundles; drawing water for the evening meal at the creaking well-windlasses; piling grass before the shrieking, wild-eyed stallions; cuffing the surly caravan dogs; paying off caravan-drivers; taking on new grooms; swearing, shouting, arguing, and chaffering in the packed square.' Such, then, was the world of Kim's friend, the wealthy Afghan horse-dealer Mahbub Ali. It was here, amidst all this turmoil, that he was to be found when he was not away buying horses in 'that mysterious land beyond the Passes of the North'.

But Mahbub Ali, as we already know, and Kim half-suspected, was involved in an altogether deeper game than just the buying and selling of horses. Since the age of ten, Kim had had shadowy dealings with the big, burly Afghan with the scarlet-dyed beard. 'Sometimes', we are told, 'he would tell Kim to watch a man who had nothing whatever to do with horses: to follow him for one whole day and report every soul with whom he talked.' Kim would pass on the information to him in the evening, and Mahbub Ali would listen intently, 'without word or gesture'. At the end, the Afghan would reward him with money, or with a mouth-watering meal 'all hot from the cookshop at the head of the serai'.

That it was intrigue of some kind, Kim knew. What he did not know was that Mahbub Ali was one of the finest, and most trusted, secret agents of the British Indian intelligence service – a veteran player in the Great Game against the Russians and other foes of the British in India. On the secret payroll of Colonel Creighton, the Raj intelligence chief, he was identified simply as C25 IB – or C25 for short. Others of Creighton's team of hand-picked native agents sheltered behind similar numbers, as we shall see, and operated under various guises – for it was a highly dangerous game they played – wherever trouble was brewing, whether inside India or beyond her frontiers. Creighton himself purported to work for the Survey of India, a genuine organisation, whose task it was to produce maps of the whole of British India and its surrounding territories, including Central Asia.

It is not difficult to see why Kipling uses the Survey as the cover for Creighton's secret operations. At the time the events in *Kim* are supposed to have taken place (although Kipling is deliberately vague about this) there was still no formal intelligence-gathering service in India. However, the Survey of India did have a clandestine side to it, as Kipling would have known. Where it was too perilous for British officers to work, especially beyond India's northern frontiers, specially trained native explorers were employed to gather topographical intelligence, often in the guise of traders or holy men on pilgrimages. Known to their Survey chiefs as 'pundits', they were given code-names such as A-K, or G-M, to protect their identities. It seems highly likely that much of the Great Game element in *Kim* was inspired by the activities of the 'pundits'.

But to return to Kim and the lama as they enter the crowded Kashmir Serai in search of Mahbub Ali, and a place for the night on his floor. Weaving their way past travellers of many races and tongues, they finally came upon the Afghan in the space he rented under the arches of the serai, near to the railway station. They found him lazing on a carpet, puffing at an enormous silver hookah, or water-pipe. The horse-dealer was startled to see Kim with the Tibetan and, after an exchange of good-natured raillery, enquired what he was up to. Kim explained that he was now the lama's *chela*, and that they were about to embark together on a pilgrimage to the holy city of Benares (today Varanasi), searching for a sacred river as they journeyed. Then, out of the old man's hearing, he added: 'He is quite mad, and I am tired of Lahore city. I wish new air and water.'

As it happened, Kim's news could hardly have come at a better moment for Mahbub Ali. For he had just returned hastily from the far north bearing a red-hot piece of intelligence – beside which, Kipling tells us, 'dynamite was milky and innocuous'. It was vital that this should be passed on to Colonel Creighton as swiftly as possible. Yet he knew that, even now, he was being shadowed by men hell-bent on preventing him from doing so. His caravan had already been attacked twice on its way down to Lahore, and his pursuers would certainly not rule out murder to retrieve the damning evidence against their masters that he was carrying. This, we learn, implicated 'five confederated Kings, who had no business to confederate', a 'sympathetic Northern Power, a Hindu banker in Peshawur, a firm of gun-makers in Belgium, and an important, semi-independent Mohammedan ruler to the south'. Such was the stuff of nightmares to the Raj authorities – a conspiracy between treacherous foes within, and an outside power, namely Tsarist Russia, 'the great deliverer from the North'.

This sudden and unexpected arrival of his young friend, Mahbub Ali realised, was a monumental piece of luck. For Colonel Creighton's headquarters was at the British garrison town of Umballa, nearly 200 miles away to the south-east. It lay on the railway to Benares, whither Kim had just announced that he and the lama were shortly going. Mahbub Ali decided to press Kim into service on the spot. Aware that they were almost certainly under close scrutiny, he whispered to Kim to act as though he was begging, by stretching out his cupped hands towards him. Long used to the mysterious ways of his Afghan friend, Kim obeyed, while Mahbub Ali briefed him. His top-secret task, for which he would be well rewarded, was to deliver a small but very important package 'of closely folded tissue-paper, wrapped in oilskin' with five microscopic pin-holes in one corner, to a certain British officer, whose house and appearance Mahbub Ali carefully described, at Umballa.

The package, he told Kim, contained the pedigree of a valuable horse which he had recently sold to that officer, who was anxiously awaiting it. So that Kim could identify himself as Mahbub Ali's emissary, and also know that he was delivering the package into the right hands, the horse-dealer gave him a spoken message, and the reply he was to expect. Finally he slipped the package to Kim, discreetly hidden in a large flap of Indian bread, together with three silver rupees – 'enormous largesse' to Kim. For the benefit of any eavesdroppers, he added that he and the old lama could go and sleep among the horse-boys, and perhaps be found some work in the morning. Kim, backing gratefully away like a beggar, did not for a moment believe the story of the pedigree. But he knew, from the generosity of the reward he had been given, that he had been entrusted with a very important mission, which added greatly to its excitement.

Its importance was alarmingly confirmed in the early hours of the following morning, when Kim awoke to see a shadowy figure going methodically through Mahbub Ali's saddle-bags and other possessions, clearly searching for something. It instantly occurred to him that the man was looking for the small package which Mahbub Ali had entrusted to him, and which was now concealed in the amulet-case hung around his neck. Meanwhile, unknown to Kim, a similar search for the package was being conducted in a house of ill-repute by the Gate of the Harpies. For that night Mahbub Ali had deliberately visited a woman there whom he knew to be friendly with one of his shadowy watchers. Pretending to get drunk on 'perfumed brandy against the Law of the Prophet', he finally collapsed unconscious among the cushions, where 'the Flower of Delight' and a 'smooth-faced Kashmiri' searched him from head to foot, albeit in vain.

Though unaware of this, Kim had already seen enough. 'Those who search bags with knives', he reasoned, 'may presently search bellies with knives.' It was clearly the moment for them to leave, before suspicion attached itself to them. Kim awakened the lama, telling him that it was time they left for Benares. Then together they slipped out of the sleeping serai 'like shadows' – a favourite phrase of Kipling's – and made their way across the darkened square towards the railway station. And there we shall part company with them for a while, as we explore other matters.

*

The tough but attractive figure of Mahbub Ali, we learn from two reliable but separate sources, appears to have been modelled on an actual Afghan horse-dealer bearing that name, who was known personally to Kipling when he was working as a young frontier journalist on the *Civil and Military Gazette*. Kay Robinson, his editor there in 1886 and 1887, when Kipling left Lahore to join the *Pioneer* in Allahabad, remembers Mahbub Ali as a Pathan of 'magnificent mien and features'. Whenever he arrived in Lahore he would call on his friend 'Kuppeleen Sahib', bringing him word of the latest goings-on beyond the Khyber Pass, in the untamed and then little-known Afghan hinterland.

Our other witness to Mahbub Ali's real-life origins is General Sir George MacMunn, the Raj military historian, who knew Lahore as an Indian Army subaltern in the 1890s. Mahbub Ali's father – 'an honourable Kabuli horse-thief', he tells us – accompanied the ill-fated 1839 British military expedition to Afghanistan, better known as the First Afghan War. Unable to return to Afghanistan afterwards, for fear of his life, he set up as a horse-dealer in Lahore with his son – Mahbub Ali 'of *Kim* fame'. They sold polo ponies, horses and mules, MacMunn records in his book *Rudyard Kipling: Craftsman*, to 'all and sundry', including British officers and the Indian Army itself.

Mahbub Ali, he goes on, had three sons – Wazir, Afzul and Aslam – who eventually inherited their father's thriving business. This was to be found in Lahore's Sultan Serai, which appears to have been part of, or even another name for, the Kashmir Serai of *Kim*. In fact, as I was shortly to discover, the Sultan Serai still exists today, though as a pale shadow of what it must have been like in MacMunn's and Kipling's time, when the horse still ruled the roads and passes of northern India. Writing in 1938, MacMunn recalls: 'If you turn into the Sultan Serai you will pass under an ancient gateway into the part frequented by Afghan traders, where used to sit the sons of Mahbub Ali.' Then, rows of horses were tethered in the yard, or under the arched recesses of the serai walls. But they no longer included the great Central Asian breeds – the Turcomans, Badakshanis and Kandaharis – for by then their export had been forbidden by the Emir of Afghanistan. One of Mahbub Ali's grandsons, MacMunn tells us, was sent to Cambridge to study veterinary science, but was unhappy there and soon returned to Lahore. Finally, Mahbub Ali's sons fell out, and the business broke up. 'Young Aslam, who is now old Aslam,' the general adds, would sometimes visit him and talk sorrowfully of 'the fallen family of Mahbub Ali'.

Although they are all now long gone – including Mac-Munn himself, and probably even Mahbub Ali's grandsons – I hoped that somewhere in the old horse bazaar area I might still find some trace, some echo, some ghost of the scarlet-bearded Afghan horse-dealer immortalised by his young friend 'Kuppeleen Sahib' in *Kim*. Dr Anjum Rehmani, the director of the museum, had explained to me where I would find what remained of the old Sultan Serai. From the busy station square, with its rickety, wheezing buses and taxis, its motor-bicycles carrying four, even five, passengers pillion, and its slow-moving country carts bearing entire families, I made my way down a side street towards the area which Dr Rehmani had circled on my map. What I hoped to find first of all was the ancient gateway described by General MacMunn, for then I would know that I was getting close to where, in Kipling's mind at least, Kim had been briefed by Mahbub Ali, master-spy of the North-West Frontier, for his first major Great Game mission.

Soon the tumult of shrieking horns and squealing tyres in the square behind me faded into the distance as I elbowed my way through the crowded Landa Bazaar. It was somewhere very near here that the Flower of Delight entertained Mahbub Ali by the Gate of the Harpies, which was most probably the nearby Delhi Gate. I next entered a maze of narrow lanes, hushed and deserted save for the odd woman in an all-enveloping black *burka* hurrying home with her shopping, and a cluster of young Kims playing alley cricket with a broken bat. I walked on, past mysterious-looking passageways and heavily padlocked doors, looking for any signs of the old horse bazaar. Once I pressed myself against a crumbling wall to allow a bullock-cart, overflowing with indescribable filth, to squeeze narrowly by me while I held my breath and fought off the escort of flies.

So far, and I had been searching for twenty minutes, I had not come across MacMunn's ancient gateway to the Sultan Serai, from which I had hoped to get my bearings. Nor had I seen so much as a single horse. But then, just as I was beginning to despair, assuming that the gateway must long ago have been knocked down, I suddenly spotted it. It lay at the end of a litter-strewn turning to my right. Its original wooden gates, now badly decayed, were still there. Excited by my discovery, I stood beneath it, wondering 'where used to sit the sons of Mahbub Ali'. If only I had the old general with me, I mused, to steer me through this labyrinth of lanes and alleyways, each looking much like the last.

Repeating slowly to myself MacMunn's words – 'If you turn into the Sultan Serai you will pass under an ancient gateway . . . Rows of horses are tethered in the yard, or under the arched recesses of the serai walls' – I began to explore the little streets around the gateway. But after another ten minutes or so there was no sign of a horse. I was determined not to give up, however, and moments later I was rewarded. As I rounded a corner my heart leaped. For there, tethered to an iron ring, stood a solitary white horse. Of its owner there was no sign, but I knew now that I was hot on the trail. It was all beginning to come true. Where there was one horse (nag would perhaps have been a more accurate description) there must be others. And with luck I might find someone who knew if any descendants or traces of 'the fallen family of Mahbub Ali' had survived. For my earlier enquiries, elsewhere in Lahore, had drawn a blank.

Continuing along the dusty lane – called Charagh Deen street, if I got it down correctly – I first came upon a stretch of little back-street garages, surrounded by bits of abandoned engines, where men were tinkering with elderly-looking cars. Had I come here fifty years too late, I began to wonder. Perhaps, with polo-playing British officers long departed, and cavalry now replaced by tanks, the horse bazaar had gone for ever, to be succeeded by men who dealt instead in cars. Just as I was beginning to lose heart once more, I suddenly spotted a row of brightly painted tongas – the two-wheeled horse-drawn carriage still used widely today – lined up along a wall. Their shafts were empty, but I felt that their horses could not be very far away. And so it proved. Peering through an entranceway to an inner courtyard, I counted sixteen horses quietly munching greenery in their stalls, while another was being hosed down until its coat shone.

It was a great moment. Was it just possible, I wondered, that this ancient-looking but clearly well-run stable was Mahbub Ali's one-time lair, albeit today in others' hands? There were three grooms busily at work on the horses, and I asked them whether they knew the name Mahbub Ali. I watched their faces carefully, and repeated his name slowly, as well as those of his three sons. But all three smiled politely and shook their heads. It was clear that the names meant nothing to them. In the street outside was a saddler, selling pieces of equestrian tack from his stall. I asked him if he knew the name Mahbub Ali, but he, too, shook his head. In a wistful moment, however, I bought from him a chromium-plated 'bit' as a reminder of the now all-but-vanished world of the Afghan horse-dealer. For even if this old-fashioned stable, hidden away in the old serai, never belonged to Mahbub Ali, I knew that his own would have looked very similar.

Sadly, the horse bazaar, which is conjured up so vividly for us in *Kim*, is not the only thing to have vanished from the Lahore that Kipling knew so intimately. The handsome old building of the *Civil and Military Gazette*, suppressed by

Field Marshal Ayub Khan's government in 1963, has long since been demolished to make way on the Mall for new developments. The Kipling family bungalow, to which this teenage genius would return in the early hours after his nocturnal walkabouts around the old city, has also gone, as has Nila Ram's timber yard near the Punjab High Court (though that still stands), where Kim kept hidden his Hindu urchin's set of clothing. For the 'fragrant deodar logs' no longer float down the Ravi river from the north for seasoning in Lahore, and Nila Ram, had he really existed, would have long ago fled to India, being a Hindu. Vanished, too, and for the same reason, are the 'ash-smeared' fakirs who lived under the trees down by the river, with whom Kim was on friendly terms. They would either have fled or been slaughtered during the nightmare of bloodletting which followed India's partition in 1947, and which was nowhere worse than in the Punjab. 'Today,' Dr Rehmani informed me, 'there are very few Hindus living in Lahore.'

*

We must now get back to Kim and the lama as they slip away from the serai and enter the railway station. For Kim fears lest it dawn on Mahbub Ali's foes that the documents they appear so desperate to get their hands on have been entrusted secretly to him. In *Kim* we are given a brilliant picture of Lahore station in the early hours of the morning – a description which, a century or so later, still more or less holds good. 'They entered the fort-like railway station,' Kipling writes, 'black in the end of night: the electrics sizzling over the goods-yard where they handle the heavy Northern grain-traffic.' Gazing up in awe at the huge steel girders supporting the roof above them, and unsettled by the 'hollow echoing darkness' of the great building, the old man can merely gasp: 'This is the work of devils.' Already the station is overflowing with third-class passengers waiting, like Kim and the lama, for the 3.25 a.m. night express to Benares. As they lie stretched out asleep they look – a favourite Kipling image this – like 'the sheeted dead'.

Kim now lets slip that they are going no further than Umballa, where, though the lama is unaware of this, he has to deliver Mahbub Ali's mysterious package. 'But we go to Benares,' protests the old man. 'All one,' Kim assures him. At that moment the train thunders in, making the lama start. 'The sleepers', writes Kipling, 'sprang to life, and the station filled with clamour and shoutings, cries of water and sweet-meat vendors, shouts of native policemen, and shrill yells of women gathering up their baskets, their families, and their husbands.' The lama is visibly alarmed by this sudden pandemonium around him, but Kim reassures him. 'It is the train – only the *te-rain*. It will not come here,' he says. Then, clutching the lama's purse, he runs across to the booking office to buy their tickets. Here we must leave them for a while, for Kipling's account of their railway journey to Umballa in a crowded compartment is a real gem which I would not dare to paraphrase. Instead, I determined to re-enact their journey myself, and find out just how much – if at all – things had changed.

# 4

# 'The Te-rain'

M Y FIRST BLOW was the discovery, while still in London, that there is no longer a 3.25 a.m. night express from Lahore to Umballa. Although disappointing, I confess that this did not come as any great surprise. After all, if Kim was born in 1865, then we are talking about a rail journey made in 1878, well over a century ago. Of course, there may never have been a 3.25 a.m. train – something which could, no doubt, be verified from a contemporary timetable. However Kipling, who never lost his reporter's eye for detail, was not given to inventing things unnecessarily. Moreover, he goes on to explain just why there was a train at so ungodly an hour. 'All hours are alike to Orientals,' he writes in *Kim*, 'and their passenger traffic is regulated accordingly.' Furthermore, I was astonished to discover that another train which features in a later chapter of the novel does still run at precisely the same time today as it did then.

I was well aware from the start, of course, that my journey in Kim and the lama's footsteps would not be as simple as in their day. For a start it involves crossing a highly sensitive frontier, on either side of which the appalling things which happened there in 1947 are neither forgotten nor forgiven, and probably never will be. I knew, moreover, that the vast majority of people making the crossing either way go by bus, car or taxi, since this is considerably quicker. To go by train, especially as a foreigner, is distinctly eccentric, as was repeatedly pointed out to me when I got there. However, like Kim and the lama, I had no choice, even if I was spared from having to leave at 3.25 a.m.

The Thomas Cook overseas railway timetable, which I consulted in London and from which I had discovered that there was no longer a night train to Umballa, informed me instead that there was now a daily train departing at 11.30 a.m. As this was the sole train of the day, I thought it wise to double check, especially when I noticed that the Lonely Planet guidebook gave the departure time as 11 a.m. I therefore faxed a travel agent I knew in Islamabad, pointing out these discrepancies, and asking him to give me the correct departure time so that I could, if he thought it necessary, reserve a seat. Replying very promptly, he informed me that there was *no* daily train to Umballa (Ambala on today's maps) from Lahore, merely a twice-weekly one leaving on Mondays and Thursdays at 11 a.m. He added, as a cautionary note perhaps, that 'we have never used this train'.

The discovery that the train was now only twice-weekly was annoying, since it gave me less flexibility when I got to Lahore. Moreover, in the face of so much conflicting intelligence about a journey of less than 200 miles, I thought it wise to check yet again. This time I decided to get it straight from the horse's mouth by ringing Lahore railway station, whose number – 92 42 320 271 – I obtained from international directory enquiries. But despite repeated attempts to get through – I must have tried at least a hundred times over a period of a week – I always got what appeared to be an engaged signal. The true explanation for this I discovered later.

I was now getting worried, for my departure to Pakistan was imminent and I was no closer to discovering what I needed to know. I attempted to fax a friend of mine, a very senior figure in the Pakistan government, but his machine appeared to be switched off. Having now tried everything, I decided that I had no choice but to go straight to Lahore railway station on my arrival and ask there. At least then I could be sure of getting the correct information, and make my plans accordingly.

*

There can be few such bloodstained railway stations in the world as that of Lahore, though the Pakistan Tourist Development Corporation may be forgiven for not drawing attention to its tragic but horrific past. Originally built by the British in 1864, only seven years after the Indian Mutiny, the station was designed also to serve as a fortress, lest it ever become necessary to defend it, either against an outside invader, which meant the Russians or the Afghans, or against the 'enemy within', meaning that perpetual Raj nightmare, a second Indian Mutiny. Looking more like a medieval castle, with its massive crenellated walls and corner towers, than a railway station, it was constructed, in the words of its architect, 'to be perfectly defensible in every aspect'. Jan

Morris, in her celebration of Raj architecture *Stones of Empire*, informs us that 'the picturesque arches through which the trains entered or left the station could be closed with heavy doors, turning the whole building into a huge bunker', and that the four corner towers were designed to be 'bomb-proof'. No wonder the lama was overwhelmed by its 'hollow echoing darkness' when he entered this great sepulchral structure.

Nor is the word sepulchral entirely inappropriate. For during the appalling massacres which swept through the Punjab following its partition in August 1947, the building was to witness some of the most ghastly scenes of all, as vast numbers of terrified Hindus, Sikhs and Muslims fled by train in a massive two-way migration. The Hindus and Sikhs were desperately trying to escape eastwards into that part of the

Punjab, including Amritsar, Umballa and Delhi, awarded to India, while the Muslims were fleeing westwards into the new Pakistan. Because the roads across the Punjab were considered to be even more dangerous, at first the refugees from either side put their trust in the, until then, British-run railways. But very soon these were being attacked by fanatical armed mobs of either side, who bribed or coerced their drivers into halting their trains at remote spots, where the passengers would then be slaughtered to the last man, woman and child.

As the hour of Independence approached, and hatreds intensified, trains began to reach Lahore crammed with the freshly dead Muslim victims of these murderous attacks, their blood seeping from beneath the doors of literally every compartment. The carriages had to be hosed down, and the corpses carried away on luggage-trolleys for mass burial, before the trains could begin their return journey, this time carrying fleeing Hindus and Sikhs. One witness to the carnage was Louis Heren, then the India correspondent of *The Times*, and who had served in the Army in India during the Second World War. He describes in his memoirs, *Growing up on the Times*, coming across a train in a siding at Amritsar which had been attacked by Sikhs while carrying Muslim refugees to Lahore. 'Every man, woman and child on board was killed, altogether about 4,000 souls,' he wrote, adding: 'I was physically sick . . .' Not long before he had been on a refugee train bound for Lahore when it was attacked by Sikhs – 'huge men heaving with excitement and breathlessness', their swords dripping with blood. Many of those on board were slaughtered, while others fled into the night, but the train finally reached Lahore with its surviving passengers – thanks, Heren acknowledges, to the determination and sense of duty of the Anglo-Indian driver and crew.

Meanwhile, in Lahore itself, Hindus and Sikhs were suffering a not dissimilar fate at the hands of vengeful Muslims. Across the city great fires were burning as temples, homes and businesses were set alight. 'It was like a city committing suicide,' recalled one British police officer, who was powerless to stop the mobs, which included some of his own Muslim officers. In *Freedom at Midnight*, an epic account of the partitioning of India, Larry Collins and Dominique Lapierre describe the scene in Lahore: 'Almost a hundred thousand Hindus and Sikhs were trapped inside old Lahore's walled city, their water cut off, fires raging around them, mobs of Muslims stalking the alleys outside their *mahallas* waiting to pounce on anyone venturing out.' In the terrible summer heat of Lahore, so nightmarishly described by Kipling in 'The City of Dreadful Night', those besieged inside the old city were beginning to go mad from thirst. Yet so intense was the hatred that even women and children who emerged to beg for a bucket of water were mercilessly slain. From one sacred building, which had been torched by the mob, could be heard the screams of Sikhs being roasted to death inside. Nor was this bloodbath confined to Lahore. The same grim story of murderous gangs, of all three religions, on the rampage was repeated right across the Punjab, with road convoys of fleeing villagers, as well as trains, being attacked on either side of the newly announced frontier. In all, though there are no reliable figures, around a million people are thought to have died, mostly in the Punjab region.

On Independence Night – August 14, 1947 – the last of the British police officers and other officials to leave Lahore, having handed over to their Pakistani successors, made their way through the corpse-strewn streets and past blazing buildings towards the railway station. Some had even shot their polo ponies with their service revolvers rather than let them end their lives, with toast-rack ribs, pulling tongas. A train was awaiting them which would convey them to Bombay, from where they would sail for home. As they entered the station they saw railway staff grimly hosing away pools of fresh blood from the platforms. For a few hours earlier an appalling massacre had taken place in the station. The victims, some of whom still lay where they had been murdered, were a group of Hindus who had somehow managed to run the gauntlet of the mob-ruled streets and reach the station. As the Bombay Express pulled out of Lahore, in the distance all around them the British could see smoke and flames rising from the villages which had been their responsibility. Their entire life's work was being destroyed before their very eyes. Had Kipling lived for another eleven years, to the age of 82, he too might have looked on in sheer disbelief at this sudden and total breakdown of civilisation among a people he had portrayed again and again in *Kim* as being in harmony with one another, albeit under a benign British guardianship. Today, as you enter Lahore railway station, it is hard to believe that such horrifying deeds were once perpetrated there, and on so frightful a scale. Yet if ever a building deserves to be haunted, it is surely this one.

My thoughts, however, were on anything but the past as I hurried into the station, for my sole concern at that moment was to find out once and for all about trains to Umballa. With bats circling overhead in the gloom, I first made for what Kim calls 'that hole' – the ticket office – where the clerk, he informs the lama, 'will give thee a paper to take thee to Umballa'. Whether it is the same 'hole' as in Kim's day, where the young Kipling would have bought his tickets too, I doubt, as it looks far too new. But from this 'hole' I was politely directed to another, not far away, where I was told they would know when the trains left for Amritsar and Umballa. They did not, and I was again re-directed, this time to 'Upper Class Reservations', though I was determined, like Kim and the lama, to go third-class. Once more I was politely shunted on, without even having discovered whether there were still trains to Umballa.

I now made my way, as instructed, to 'Advance Reservations', which lay at the very end of one of the platforms. However, as I did so I spotted an impressive-looking, uniformed figure, with an equally impressive moustache, who appeared to be the station-master, or possibly his deputy. I asked him if he could tell me when the trains left for Umballa. He looked at me in surprise, or perhaps it was out of pity, and then somewhat ominously suggested that I would do far better to take a taxi to Amritsar, and pick up an Indian train there for the onward journey to Umballa. It was obviously pointless my explaining why I *had* to go by train, as it was highly unlikely that he had ever so much as heard of *Kim*, of which – or so one Lahore bookseller assured me – there has never been an Urdu translation. I therefore thanked him for his advice and proceeded towards 'Advance Reservations'.

The platform – number one, out of a total of eight – was running with mischievous young Kims. Every now and again one of them would dart up to the great station bell and give it a violent tug, making elderly passengers jump and bringing station staff puffing over to chase them away. Otherwise, apart from the squadrons of bats in the rafters, it was not that different from King's Cross on a Friday night. When I reached the office I was looking for, which had nothing to indicate what it was, I was greeted by a humorous individual wearing a pink spangled skull-cap who hailed me as though he was expecting me (which he wasn't). Surrounding him on his desk were scores of files, presumably recording 'Advance Reservations'. Noticing his telephone, I told him that I had tried to ring the station from London to obtain the information I now hoped to get in person. He chuckled, then told me, almost with pride, 'Telephone not been paid. Not been paid for months. It's been disconnected.' No wonder I had been unable to get through. But now, at least, I would be able to book myself a seat on Kim and the lama's train, or its nearest equivalent.

The train, he told me, went twice a week, on Mondays and Thursdays, precisely as my Islamabad travel agent had informed me, though it left at 11.30, not at 11 o'clock. At last I was getting somewhere, even if I had missed that day's train, it being Monday evening. Still, I had a lot to do first, so Thursday's train would be ideal. I now had the problem of explaining that I, a well-dressed, prosperous-looking sahib, wished to go third-class. I started by asking whether it was necessary to reserve seats on this train, as I imagined that not many people chose to go to India from Lahore, especially when relations between the two countries were so bad.

It was then, bit by bit, that the truth began to emerge. First, one could not reserve seats on this train. Second, at least a thousand people would be travelling on it, mainly visiting relatives and friends in India. If I was to stand a hope of getting on it, let alone securing a seat, I would be wise to be at the station not a minute later than 7 a.m. in order to join the ticket queue. After that there would be a long wait while a thousand people were cleared through emigration and customs. Finally, when everyone was through, there would be a free-for-all for the available seats in which I, with my lack of experience, would almost certainly lose out. Finally, instead of the advertised departure time of 11.30, the train would be unlikely to leave before 1 p.m. I would do far better, he advised, if I took a taxi across the frontier and picked up an onward train from there. This was precisely what the kindly station-master had told me ten minutes earlier, and I now saw why. But I was not that easily put off. Indeed, it sounded rather fun, despite the probable discomfort. After all, as Roger Cooper said cheerfully after five years in an Iranian gaol, if you've been to an English public school and served in the British Army you can survive virtually anything. I had done both.

But now came the really bad bit of news. *Where* was it

that I wanted to leave the train, my friend asked, as though
he had suddenly remembered something? Ambala, I replied,
being careful to use the modern name. He shook his head
slowly. 'Impossible,' he said. Because of a new Indian regu-
lation, the train was now a 'sealed' one. It was not allowed
to stop at Ambala or anywhere else, but went straight through
to Delhi. From there I would have to take a train all the
way back to Ambala. I asked him why the train was not
allowed to stop at Ambala, even to drop off foreigners. The
Indian authorities seemed to think, he told me, that Pakistani
terrorists would slip off the train there and make trouble for
them, absurd as this might appear.

Short of hurling myself off the train as it thundered
through Ambala station, it was clear that there was no way
now that I could follow exactly in Kim and the lama's footsteps. It began to emerge, moreover, that the train did not even
go via Ambala, but took a more direct route to Delhi, so I
would have to hurl myself some considerable distance if I was
going to end up on the platform at Ambala. The discovery –
despite the timetable, despite the guidebooks and despite my
travel agent friend in Islamabad – that the train no longer ran
was disappointing, for I had promised myself for years that I
would take the 'te-rain'. Perhaps one day, when the two countries have learned to live with one another, I might try again,
but for the time being I would have to settle for the taxi across
the frontier to Amritsar, where I could again pick up my
quarry's trail. As it was, I would only be missing the first thirty
miles or so of a rail journey of nearly two hundred.

However, there was a way, I discovered, of narrowing even

that gap. Several times a day a local train leaves Lahore for
the small frontier post of Waggah, through which Kim and
the lama would have passed, although then, of course, there
was no frontier. On reaching Waggah, instead of continuing
into India, the train simply turns round and comes back. By
taking this train I might be able to accompany Kim and the
lama on the first stage of their journey before turning back,
but then catch up with them again at Amritsar station by
taxi. I decided to do just that.

*

My ticket to the Indian frontier and back, a journey of two
hours, cost me just 22p. At first the clerk behind the 'hole'
had been extremely reluctant to sell me one at all, thinking
perhaps that I was a spy. After all, who else would have any
good reason for wanting to visit this highly sensitive frontier
which, during my stay in Lahore, was in the headlines – and
angry ones at that – almost daily? In the end, however, he
appeared satisfied that this strange creature who kept repeating the words 'Kim' and 'lama' and pointing to a book he
was carrying was simply an English crackpot, and he gave
me my ticket. The train – a simple, one-carriage affair which
had seen better days – was waiting at platform 8, together
with a crowd of passengers. Apart from a group of schoolboys,
most of the passengers were villagers from Waggah and other
halts along the line who had been shopping in the Lahore
bazaars. However, I soon spotted two other foreigners,
clutching large suitcases, who told me they were Iranians
working for the United Nations.

## 'The Te-rain'

As we trundled slowly through the Lahore suburbs, the young Kims hung precariously out of the windows shouting what sounded like insults at people they seemed to know in the streets below. I imagined that this was a daily ritual on the homeward run from school, for their catcalls met with long-suffering looks from their fellow passengers and no reaction whatsoever from those at whom they were directed. From the covert glances made towards where I sat, however, I could tell that today I was an interesting new addition to their regular audience. I had to fight hard not to catch their eye, for I knew that the moment I did I would be unable to suppress a smile, and that would have been fatal. So I buried my head in my book and tried to look stern. Soon the insults dried up as the boys switched to other diversions in the sweltering heat.

Apart from that the journey was uneventful. Outside stretched the flat, brown Punjab countryside, with its little market gardens, hardly changed, no doubt, since Kim's day. Boys flew kites, vultures circled lazily, bullock-carts toiled, women struggled with firewood, while all the time the heat shimmered over the dusty plain around us. Now and again we halted at a small station – Moghul Pura, Harbans Pura, Jallo or Taqipur – and several more passengers squeezed into the already overcrowded train. In this respect, too, little appeared to have changed very much since Kim, with the lama in tow, had fought his way on to the 'te-rain' (perhaps the same one, so archaic was mine) at Lahore. 'There is no room even for a mouse,' a Hindu woman had protested as Kim and the lama squeezed into her compartment. But on

my train, as on theirs, space was somehow found for the
newcomers, either sitting on the floor like the lama, or – in
the case of a stout woman plus baby – half perched on my
lap, not daring to look round.

Not long afterwards, amidst much shouting and tooting,
we halted, blessedly, at Waggah, a forlorn-looking station,
seemingly in the middle of nowhere, but which had twice
witnessed much bloodshed. In the summer of 1947, the 'death
trains' had all passed through Waggah on their way to and
from India, while in the 1965–6 India-Pakistan war it had
been in the front line of a major tank battle. But, like Lahore
railway station, it was hard to believe that such things had
once taken place here, so utterly remote and peaceful was it.
It was at Waggah that all the other passengers left the train
and began to straggle towards the village, which evidently
lay some distance away. The last I saw of the two Iranians was
of them hobbling across the fields with their heavy suitcases
towards the border-post, where they told me they were planning to cross into India on foot. Things had certainly not
got any easier since Kim's day – as I myself would discover
in due course.

My journey back to Lahore, in a half-empty train this
time, was uneventful, save for two rather curious things.
Squatting on the hard wooden seats, looking like extras from
a film on the North-West Frontier in the Great Game era,
were a number of lean, blanketed men in white turbans.
Where they had come from I had no idea, though it looked
as though they were on their way home to Pathan country.
Among the other passengers, mainly local villagers, they were

eye-catching enough. But it was one man in particular who held me transfixed throughout the journey.

If the others looked like film extras, this compelling figure had all the appearance of a 1930s film star playing a British officer in disguise. Lighter skinned than the rest, with hooded eyes, aquiline nose and sensitive features, he was strikingly handsome behind his British military-style moustache. Lean and sinewy, he squatted with a thin grey blanket wrapped around him, clearly lost in his own thoughts. While the others chatted and fidgeted, this mysterious apparition sat apart, speaking to no one, looking at no one, and never appearing to move. As we drew into Lahore I took my eyes off him for a moment, and when I looked up again he was gone, vanishing as suddenly and silently as he had come. Perhaps it was the ghost of Colonel Creighton come to look for Kim.

The only other thing of interest on that journey back from the frontier happened as I was quickly jotting down impressions in a small notebook, unaware that I was being observed. Suddenly two young men sitting nearby leaned over and one asked me, ever so politely, if I was making maps. I think it was mere inquisitiveness, but I did find myself wondering afterwards whether they had been instructed to watch me and see what I was up to on my mysterious journey to their frontier with their old foe India. Otherwise why mention maps, of all things? I happily showed them my page of notes, and told them that I was writing a book about their beautiful land. But I kicked myself afterwards for not asking them discreetly who the inscrutable, turbaned individual in the corner was.

And oh yes, before I forget. I picked up one useful tip on fare-dodging from the young Kims on my train. As we slowed down on approaching Lahore, several of them simply jumped out of the window and ran off into the darkness. No doubt Kipling's Kim, who knew a thing or two about fare-dodging, used that trick a century or more before they were born.

As I left the station for my hotel (not, I must confess, one of the raffish ones nearby), I passed along a platform at which a crowded troop-train had just arrived from Quetta on its way northwards. For obvious reasons I did not ask where it was bound for, but through the windows I could see scores of young soldiers, all appearing strangely subdued and silent. Perhaps they were merely exhausted from their very long journey. But it was not impossible that they were on their way up to Baltistan to join the long-running, forgotten war there against India for possession of the Siachin glacier, one of the few corners of the world still without properly defined ownership. At 21,000 feet, this is the highest battlefield on earth, where a man's body begins to die after only thirty days. A British reporter who visited this icy hell was told that for every soldier killed in the actual fighting, *nine* perished from frostbite, avalanches or other consequences of the nightmarish conditions. At this altitude, and in these temperatures, he wrote, 'it tests a soldier's strength even to lift his rifle', let alone to fight.

It is because of this war, which has now been going on for more than a decade, that no one has been able to reach the old Karakorum Pass (not to be confused with the modern Karakorum Highway) which once carried travellers and caravans from northern India over the mountains into Chinese Central Asia. Somewhere up there, at around 19,000 feet, there may still lie a crumbling monument marking the spot where in 1888 a young Scottish player in the Great Game named Andrew Dalgleish was murdered, together with his terrier, by a giant Afghan. It has long been my wish to try to find it, but even if the war eventually ends – and there is little sign of this at the time of writing – the area, where Pakistan, India and China meet, is likely to remain out of bounds for years to come.

By comparison, following in the footsteps of Kim and the lama was an altogether easier proposition, although even that was not without its problems, as we have seen. But now, having completed all my tasks in Lahore, I was ready to cross into India in pursuit of them. I ordered the taxi for 7 a.m.

# 5

# Searching for the Colonel's Bungalow

B Y NOW KIM and the lama were well ahead of me. At Umballa a kindly Hindu couple who had befriended them on the train gave them accommodation for the night. The following day they planned to set out in search of the River of the Arrow. But Kim, it will be recalled, had more urgent business to attend to first – the safe delivery of his friend Mahbub Ali's mysterious package to Colonel Creighton. Telling the lama that he was going to the bazaar to buy food for their journey, he set off to look for Colonel Creighton's bungalow, the whereabouts of which Mahbub Ali had carefully described to him, carrying with him, wrote Kipling, 'his own and a few score thousand other folk's fate slung around his neck'.

The house, when he came upon it, was ablaze with lights, and Kim could see servants moving between tables bearing flowers, glass and silver. Clearly there was going to be a party of some kind. Presently, as Kim watched from behind a clump of tall grass close to the veranda, there strode into the darkened garden an Englishman in a dinner jacket. The light was too poor for Kim to see whether his face fitted Mahbub Ali's description, so as he came closer Kim hissed his favourite beggar's opening line: 'Protector of the Poor!' The English-man stiffened, then backed towards him. Kim hissed again: 'Mahbub Ali says . . .'

'Hah! What says Mahbub Ali?' grunted the Englishman.

'The pedigree of the white stallion is fully established.'

'What proof is there?'

'Mahbub Ali has given me this proof.'

Kim now tossed the small package towards the English-man, who quickly covered it with his foot as a gardener came round the corner. When the man had gone, he dropped a rupee on the ground for Kim and then strode into the house, never looking back. Such then was Kim's first brief encounter with Colonel William Creighton, head of the British secret service in India, and the man who was to shape his destiny. But instead of picking up his rupee and slipping away, his mission fulfilled, Kim remained hidden in the garden. Deter-mined to see and hear more of what was going on inside, he began to worm his way closer to the mysterious bungalow. For he knew there was much more to all this than a simple horse pedigree, and this was a game which appealed strongly to his sense of adventure.

He was quickly rewarded. From where he now lay he watched the Englishman sit down and eagerly study the message he had delivered from Mahbub Ali, and which the

nocturnal intruders at the Lahore serai had been so anxious
to obtain. The Englishman's face, Kim noted, 'changed and
darkened' as, by the light of a kerosene lamp, he read further.
When a woman's voice warned him that their guests would
be here at any moment, he continued to read intently.
Clearly, Kim could see, this was no ordinary horse pedigree,
nor Mahbub Ali any ordinary horse-dealer. Five minutes
later, the woman called more urgently: 'Will! *He's* come. I
can hear the troopers in the drive.' Seconds later a horse-
drawn landau, with an escort of four Indian troopers riding
close behind it, swept by only inches from where Kim lay,
and halted before the bungalow.

From it there stepped down a tall, commanding figure.
The Englishman – we shall call him Colonel Creighton from
now on – hurriedly put down Mahbub Ali's message and
dashed outside to greet him. After speaking briefly to the
visitor in a low voice, he led him to the room where he had
been reading the Afghan agent's message. The older
man studied it closely and then said to Creighton: 'I'd
been expecting it for some time, but this clinches it.'
Although the India Council – the Viceroy's advisory body
– would be alerted, he felt that this was a case 'where one
is justified in assuming that we take action at once'. Eight
thousand men, he added, would probably be sufficient. He
instructed Creighton to signal the Rawalpindi and Peshawar
brigades.

'Then it means war?' Creighton asked.

'No. Punishment.'

'But C25 may have lied.'

'He bears out the other's information,' the older man replied. 'Send off those telegrams at once – the new code, not the old . . .' With that he hurried back to join the other guests.

Kim, excited by this talk of war, now crept round to the kitchen, where he hoped to pick up more from the servants. But he was spotted by one of them who proceeded to kick him. Feigning tears, Kim whined: 'I came only to wash dishes in return for a bellyful.' Then he added: 'It is a very big dinner.' The servant fell into the trap. This was hardly surprising, he snapped, for the guest-of-honour was none other than the *Jang-i-Lat Sahib* – the Army Commander-in-Chief. Kim had learned all he wanted. When the servant turned round again, the beggar had gone. Full of self-importance at his own role in what even he, aged thirteen, knew to be momentous events, Kim hurried back to where he and the lama were staying. 'It is big news,' he muttered to himself, hardly able to contain his excitement.

\*

Considering that Waggah is the sole crossing-point on the entire land frontier between Pakistan and India, and that the combined population of the two countries is more than one billion, I found the border-post surprisingly deserted. I had heard alarmist tales of queues half a mile long, and of the crossing taking three or four hours in the ferocious midday heat. But in the event I found myself virtually the only person crossing into India that morning. Indeed, there appeared to be more passport and customs officials either side of the strip of no man's land than travellers. Even so the crossing took me a good hour, which was spent filling in forms, answering questions (including whether I could find someone a job in London), and opening my meagre baggage for a dozen (I counted them) different officials. As it happened, I had their undivided attention, but had two crowded buses turned up at that moment it might have been a different story.

Having paid off my Pakistani taxi driver, my principal worry was whether I would be able to find another, on the Indian side, to take me to Amritsar, for both border-posts appeared to be in the middle of nowhere. With luck, a taxi might be dropping off someone on the Indian side of the frontier as I passed through. Indeed, much to my relief that is what happened, and very soon I was on my way to Amritsar, from where I hoped to catch a train for the four-hour journey, in the footsteps of Kim and the lama, to Umballa. Twice before in my life I have passed through Amritsar, but have always been in a hurry. This time I would have liked to visit the scene of the Amritsar massacre of April 1919, today a shrine to the 379 dead and 1,200 wounded of that notorious incident which followed the killing of five Englishmen during riots in the then capital of the Punjab. Twenty-one years later Sir Michael O'Dwyer, Governor of the Punjab at the time, paid for it with his life when, at a crowded meeting of the Royal Central Asian Society in London, he was gunned down by a Sikh assassin, who was later hanged. But once again I was in a hurry, for I wanted to reach Umballa that night, and could not therefore risk missing the train. So instead I headed straight for the station where I bought my ticket from a clerk who asked me whether all Indians in Britain were rich.

I had hoped that this might be a steam train, for I had just read in *The Times* that there were still 1,706 of these in service, though they were being scrapped at the rate of 100 a month and replaced by diesels. The same thing was happening in Pakistan, where tribal arms manufacturers were snapping up their rusting carcasses to melt down and turn into look-alike Kalashnikovs and other pirated weaponry. No doubt in remote backwaters of India trains like that on which Kim and the lama travelled in such genial company to Umballa still run. But mine was not one of these. Nor was it one of those portrayed in the glossy, up-market Raj-by-rail travel brochures, in which turbaned, white-uniformed flunkeys proffer iced drinks to elegantly dressed passengers. Even the addition of a steam locomotive would not have redeemed this air-conditioned diesel nightmare. The long, gloomy steel carriage, with its grim battleship-grey décor, its dingy striplighting, its cheap formica panelling, and its grimy tinted windows, might have challenged even Kipling's powers of description. I immediately abandoned any attempt, with *Kim* in hand, to recreate in my mind's eye Kipling's wonderful account of that long-ago journey, based as it was on his own intimate familiarity with the line.

However, the scenery outside, or what I could see of it through the dust-coated window, could scarcely have changed in the century and more since the young Kipling, on his way up to Simla, used to take the train from Lahore to Umballa. So flat is the great brown Punjab plain – across which British strategists once feared that invading Tsarist armies would advance – that one can travel for hours without spotting a single hill, even on the horizon. But whereas just across the frontier the villages proclaimed their faith with picturesque little mosques, here there were white wooden temples. Otherwise the country was virtually indistinguishable from that which I had left behind, with the same loess-like soil, the same toiling women, the same labouring bullocks, the same mud-brick farmsteads, and the same trees encrusted with vultures. I also noticed numerous rivers and streams, any one of which could have been the River of the Arrow. But fortunately, perhaps, the lama would not have spotted these from where he sat on the floor of his and Kim's compartment.

*

Few people today have ever heard of Umballa, let alone been there. But in the days of the Raj it was a garrison town of considerable size and importance. Located only seventy-eight miles south of Simla, by then the permanent headquarters of the British military in India, it was strategically situated on both the Grand Trunk Road, which stretched all the way from Calcutta, via Delhi, to the Khyber Pass, and the far-flung Indian railway network. From Umballa troops and artillery could be moved quickly to crush trouble anywhere in northern India, whether a Russian or Afghan invasion, or an uprising among the frontier tribes. For the same reason, no doubt, Kipling based Colonel Creighton at Umballa rather than at Simla, where he would have been less conveniently placed for his shadowy travels around India. Before the railway was built up to Simla, one had a twelve-hour journey south by tonga every time one ventured down from the hills, and a much slower one on one's return. Yet, as we have seen, Creighton maintained close contact with the Commander-in-Chief, who was based in Simla, either by coded telegraph or in person.

In Creighton's day the garrison consisted of one British and one Indian infantry regiment, one British and one Indian cavalry regiment, and three batteries of artillery. Umballa had a population of 50,000 people, of whom just over half were connected in one way or another with the military establishment. They all lived in the cantonments, which covered some thirty square miles, and lay four miles from the town itself. In the centre were the residential quarters of the officers and their families, while beyond them were the military lines. All were well shaded by trees of the *Ficus religiosa* species, or so my 1883 Murray's guide tells me. It also informs me that the garrison church, built by an officer in the Bengal Engineers and consecrated in 1857, was 'one of the finest, if not the finest church in India', and was designed to accommodate 1,000 worshippers. Sadly, St Paul's Church is now in ruins – not the victim of neglect, but of a direct hit during the Pakistan-India war of 1965–6, for it stood in the heart of the old British cantonments, which the Indian Army had inherited at the time of independence.

My main aim in Umballa was to try to find Colonel Creighton's bungalow, or one whose appearance most closely matched that described in *Kim*. For it was not entirely impossible that Kipling had a particular one in mind when, some years after leaving India for good, he sat down to describe it. He even gave it a name – Laurel Bank – as we know from a telegram sent there by Mahbub Ali. If it was

based on an actual bungalow, then it might well lie fairly close to the railway station. For it was here that Kipling used to alight whenever he travelled up to Simla, whether coming from Lahore or, later, from Allahabad. It seems unlikely that he would have ventured very far into the cantonments, for they would have been superficially no different from those at Lahore. It was with this in mind that I set out to look for the bungalow in whose garden Kim had spied on

Creighton and the Commander-in-Chief of the Indian Army.

Because this was still a military area, in a country, more-over, which was virtually at war with its neighbour, I realised that I must proceed cautiously, lest I be arrested as a spy, as had happened to me elsewhere. After all, no self-respecting interrogator could be expected to swallow my story – that I was looking for the home of a spy-master who never really existed outside the pages of fiction. I decided, therefore, to go in search of the bombed Anglican church, which I knew lay in the middle of the cantonment area, and which was just the sort of thing that a nostalgic Englishman might be expected to do. Provided I did not find it too soon, this would give me the chance to inspect the bungalows on the way there from the station.

But among the scores of newish bungalows I passed there was not one that even remotely resembled Colonel Creighton's. Then, all of a sudden, I spotted something else. It looked totally out of place here, in the heart of the Punjab. Among the trees in the distance, its stonework glowing warmly in the setting sun, was the unmistakable sight of an English church tower. It appeared, from where I stood, to be intact, with its four slim finials still pointing heavenwards. By a happy chance, before leaving London, I had come upon an old picture postcard of the church. With its Victorian Gothic architecture, its elaborate covered gateway and low perimeter wall, it would not have been out of place in any small English market town. Clearly it was intended to remind the men of home.

For a moment, as I walked towards it, I wondered whether

perhaps I had been misinformed about the bombing, now thirty years ago, or had even got the wrong church. But then, as I came closer, I saw the whole of the building – or rather what now remained of it. Although the handsome tower was still standing, with much of its ornament undamaged, the nave had been totally devastated. It was clear that this was where the Pakistan Air Force bomb had hit the church, demolishing most of the exterior wall and bringing down the entire roof. The rubble had long ago been cleared away, and the great ruin made secure. Although it stood alone on a piece of wasteland, overlooked by no other buildings, I was impressed to see on its crumbling stonework no sign of graffiti or other vandalism. But then I was in the middle of a garrison town where regimental silver dating from Raj days, and other past treasures, are still lovingly preserved, including the portraits, in silver frames, of former British officers. Where that degree of respect for the past survives, some of it, no doubt, rubs off on the young of military families.

I was sad to leave this poignant spot, which in death had taken on a peculiar beauty. Half a century ago British soldiers had worshipped an alien God here – always carrying their arms into church so that never again would they be surprised by 'the enemy within', as in the Indian Mutiny. A few of those soldiers, now very old, might still remember the church parades at St Paul's, in temperatures sometimes soaring to a hellish 110 degrees on the old Fahrenheit thermometer. Few, if any, Britons have reason to visit Umballa nowadays, and very likely I was the first to gaze at the ruined church in years. An hour before it had merely served as a cover for the search for Creighton's bungalow, but it had now taken me over. In leaving it I felt a sense almost of betrayal at turning my back on this silent and disturbing memorial to a now long-vanished empire which I too had once served, though on a different frontier, on another continent.

I had stayed much longer than I intended, for the sun was now dipping behind the trees. Although my search for the bungalow seemed, momentarily anyway, a little frivolous, I still hoped to find it while daylight lasted. I took a different route back to the railway station, passing scores of small look-alike bungalows in the tree-lined avenues which criss-crossed the cantonment area. But none of them was remotely like, or indeed old enough to be, Laurel Bank. There was little point, I thought, in searching for a bungalow of that name. Most of them appeared to have numbers only, though those of some senior officers had signs at the gateway stating their name and rank. Despite their benevolence towards their British predecessors, it seemed unlikely that the name of Laurel Bank would have been preserved all these years, even if it had once existed. Just why Kipling chose to call it that in the first place is a little baffling, though perhaps some Kipling scholar can explain. It was just possible, however, that this was the name of an actual bungalow belonging to a friend of his, which he had in mind when he wrote those two pages of *Kim*. It was this remote possibility which kept me going, and very soon I found myself rewarded.

The bungalow which caught my eye was older and larger than those around it. It stood on a corner, set slightly apart from the others. It was painted white, with pale blue shutters, and had a short driveway and a somewhat overgrown garden which had seen better days. It stood only a few minutes' walk from the station, though I had reached it by a somewhat roundabout route. The house was surrounded by a low wall, over which Kim could easily have slipped, while the garden nurtured sufficient vegetation for him to have hidden behind while eavesdropping on Creighton and his guest from Simla.

There was no sign whatsoever of any laurel bushes, however, nor did the bungalow appear to have a name.

Nailed to a post in the garden, though, was a wooden board bearing the name Colonel —— ——. I have deliberately omitted his name lest his bungalow become a shrine for *Kim* fans, for which the colonel might not thank me. Indeed, he might even have them all arrested for trespassing, or behaving highly suspiciously, on what is presumably military property. I should, of course, have boldly rung the colonel's door-bell – as I would have done without hesitation more than thirty years ago when I worked for the old *Daily Express* in the Beaverbrook era – and asked him outright if his house had ever been called Laurel Bank. I might even have asked him, for good measure, whether he was head of the Indian intelligence services, whereupon he would have had me arrested – always a good story in the high days of Fleet Street. But twenty years on *The Times* must have made me more timorous, or perhaps more civilised. I decided against it, so will now never know whether this was once Creighton's house, albeit in the mind of Rudyard Kipling.

But if I had failed signally to solve the mystery of Colonel Creighton's bungalow, there still remained the mystery of the man himself. On what real-life individual, if any, did Kipling model his shadowy head of the Raj secret service? He himself gives us few clues – fittingly, perhaps, in view of Creighton's job. Mahbub Ali, it may be recalled, described his physical appearance to Kim, so that he would be able to recognise him, though Kipling was careful not to pass this on to the reader. All that he tells us, and in brackets at that, is that 'Mahbub here described the house and the appearance of the officer' to his secret emissary. It is a classic example of the 'need to know' principle. Kim did, the reader does not. But gradually, as the story unfolds, more clues emerge, until eventually it becomes virtually certain who the real-life inspiration for Creighton was. However, I shall not finally unmask him until we have more of that evidence in our hands.

There is one identification, though, which we can now attempt – that of Creighton's nocturnal visitor, the British

Commander-in-Chief, whom Kim heard giving the order for war (or punishment, as he insisted) to be unleashed against 'the five confederated Kings' after reading Mahbub Ali's damning report on their treachery. We can be reasonably confident, I think, that he is modelled on Field Marshal Lord Roberts of Kandahar, VC, who was Commander-in-Chief of the Indian Army between 1885 and 1893, overlapping with Kipling's years in India. He was, moreover, one of Kipling's few heroes – a man whom many considered to be the finest soldier in the British Army since the Duke of Wellington – and they were to become lifelong friends.

Years after Roberts's death, Kipling wrote that the proudest moment in his life was when, as a young reporter of only twenty-two, he rode alone with him along the Mall at Simla, being questioned by the great man about the mood of the Indian Army, and what the men were really talking about in the barracks. 'I told him, and he thanked me as gravely as though I had been a full Colonel,' Kipling recalled in *Something of Myself*, his posthumously published memoir, and the nearest he ever got to writing an autobiography. In view of this, it seems very likely that he would have had Roberts in mind when he wrote that scene. Further corroboration of this emerges later in the book when it transpires that the fictional Commander-in-Chief had been, early in his career, a subaltern in the Bengal Artillery – just as Roberts once was.

And if one still needs to be convinced, one should consider the fictional Commander-in-Chief's insistence that it was punishment, not war, that he proposed to mete out to the rebellious northern chiefs, since the remark is full of significance. For in the summer of 1879, only three years before Kipling's arrival in Lahore, and at the height of the Great Game, a sensational and horrifying piece of news had reached Roberts, then a general, in Simla. It had been delivered, in a manner somewhat reminiscent of Mahbub Ali's message, by a native agent who had just ridden hot-foot to the Afghan-Indian frontier from Kabul, from where it had been telegraphed to Simla.

Sir Louis Cavagnari, the British Resident in Kabul, together with two other Britons – one the holder of the Victoria Cross – and their entire, seventy-strong Corps of Guides escort, had been slaughtered by mutinous Afghan troops after a desperate but vain defence of the Residency. It was a repeat performance of the massacre there, some forty years earlier, of a previous Resident, Sir Alexander Burnes, his two British companions, one of them his brother, and their thirty-strong sepoy escort. That massacre had gone unpunished. Indeed 16,000 more Britons and Indians – soldiers, families and servants – had been slaughtered in the passes in the subsequent evacuation of Kabul.

This time, however, it was different. Roberts, who had dined with his friend Cavagnari the night before his departure for Kabul, personally led a punitive expedition into Afghanistan, sweeping all before him and quickly occupying Kabul. The Viceroy, Lord Lytton, had toyed with the idea of burning the Afghan capital to the ground as a punishment, but instead Roberts rounded up the ringleaders and others suspected of being behind the murders, and hanged nearly a hundred of them on a row of gallows facing the spot where Cavagnari and his comrades had died. Roberts was strongly criticised in the liberal press and in Parliament for his summary justice. But Afghanistan, although always a worry, was to give no further trouble until the First World War when German agents tried unsuccessfully, though only just, to unleash the ferocity of the Afghan tribal armies in a holy war against British India, the full story of which I have told elsewhere.

If Kipling's fictional Commander-in-Chief is modelled on Roberts, one can see why, in his overheard conversation with Creighton, he makes such a point about it being 'punishment' and not war. For not only did Roberts himself use that same word to justify the invasion of Afghanistan, but he also warned Cavagnari's murderers that he was coming to wreak 'public vengeance' and exact 'full retribution' from them for their treachery. For such talk nowadays he would, no doubt, be dismissed from the army. In fact, he was awarded a baronetcy, later rising to become a Field Marshal and receiving an earldom. I was interested to see, incidentally, that it was from Umballa that he set out on his punitive expedition.

*

Having found the only bungalow in the Umballa cantonments even vaguely answering to Kipling's description of Creighton's home, I caught a motorised rickshaw back to my hotel. 'The worst hotels in the world are those in India,' declared Eliza Scidmore, a seasoned American traveller, in 1903. Certainly things have improved since then, for India now has some of the finest. My hotel in Umballa, however, was not one of them, though the less said about its short-comings the better, for Indians are notoriously litigious. Indeed, court actions sometimes continue over several generations, and I would not wish that upon my children or their children. However, my discomforts that night were more than made up for by the exhilaration of knowing that the following morning I would be setting off along the Grand Trunk Road in the footsteps of Kim and the lama as they searched for the River of the Arrow – and also, as we shall see, for a Red Bull on a green field.

# 6

# The Red Bull

W HEN KIM RETURNED from his evening's adventure
at the bungalow of Colonel Creighton, bursting with
excitement and self-importance at what he had just overheard, he found the lama and their kindly hosts discussing
horoscopes with the family priest. Never one to be left out,
Kim immediately asked about his own horoscope, and his
father's prophecy about a Red Bull. Truth to tell, until meeting the lama, he had never given much thought to the opium-
fuddled tale about how one day he would be honoured by
'nine hundred first-class devils, whose God was a Red Bull
on a green field'. However, on learning of the lama's mysterious search for the River of the Arrow, Kim had decided that
he too, as his *chela*, must have a quest.

Kim remembered one further detail of his father's story,
which he told the priest – that 'first will come the two
men making ready the ground for these matters'. Having

established Kim's hour and date of birth – which had coincided with a long-remembered earthquake in Kashmir – the priest took a twig and began to draw curious patterns in the dust. Finally, after much muttering and deliberation, he turned to Kim and declared: 'Within three days come the two men to make all things ready. After them follows the Bull.' He also saw in Kim's stars hundreds of armed men. 'Thine', he told him, 'is a red and angry sign of war to be loosed very soon.' In view of what he already knew, this was no surprise to Kim, to whom the strange world of Mahbub Ali and Colonel Creighton, even if he could not quite fathom what it was all about, was becoming increasingly intriguing.

The following morning Kim and the lama continued their search for the sacred river, turning aside to explore every stream along the way. That evening found them in a mud-walled village whose hospitable headman gave them a meal and shelter for the night. Here they met an old soldier who had been a native officer at the time of the Mutiny, and whom the British had rewarded for his loyalty. Kim, who loved nothing more than to be the centre of attention, began to vaunt his inside knowledge of the coming war, though he was careful to dress it up in the mumbo-jumbo of prophecy he had picked up from the fakirs in Lahore. Immediately he was challenged by the old soldier, who pointed out that there were always wars going on along the frontier. 'But this shall be a great war,' shrilled Kim, his voice beginning to attract a small crowd, 'a war of eight thousand. From Pindi to Peshawur they will be drawn.' The old soldier now demanded that Kim give 'a sign' of some kind to prove his dubious tale. Drawing on what he had seen of the Commander-in-Chief at the bungalow, Kim described 'the man in whose hands these things lie', whom he had seen in his vision giving orders for war. So accurate was his description that the old soldier, who had seen him 'in the smoke of battles', rose stiffly to his feet and saluted. 'Enough,' he said. 'I believe . . . It is He!'

Kim's reputation as a prophet was now made, and he spent that night listening to the old man's 'tales of the Mutiny and young captains thirty years in their graves', before dropping off exhausted. Here, if one reads Kipling's sentence carefully, is an important clue to when the events in *Kim* took place, for the inference is that these young captains died in the Mutiny – that is, thirty years before. If so, our narrative begins in the year 1888, or thereabouts. Hitherto, Kipling scholars – or those of them who have considered the question – have assumed it to be ten years earlier. This assumption was based on the presumed date of Kim's birth – May 1, 1865, the same year as Kipling's – the only evidence for which is the Kashmir earthquake already referred to. Add to this the stated age of Kim when the book opens – thirteen – and we find ourselves in 1878. Unfortunately this clashes with the Second Afghan War (1878–80), of which there is not a single mention in *Kim*. It seems unlikely that Kipling would have deliberately chosen these years for a novel about the Great Game and then have ignored the principal event of that period completely.

It seems far more likely that Kim's date of birth has been wrongly arrived at, and that the clue let slip by the old soldier

is the one we should really be guided by. For it brings the
action forward to a time, after the Second Afghan War, when
there was serious trouble brewing among the northern 'kings'
– notably in Hunza, where the ruler had been having secret
dealings with that formidable Russian player in the Great
Game, Captain Gromchevsky. It was around this time, too,
that three French explorers – at first mistaken for Russians
– entered India through the Pamir passes from Tsarist Central Asia. Among those who entertained them once their
nationalities had been established was Lockwood Kipling,
though it seems unlikely that Rudyard would have met them,
as he was by then working some 600 miles away in Allahabad
for the *Pioneer*. Nonetheless, the significance of the Frenchmen's unexpected arrival to the plot of *Kim* will become
apparent in due course.

After their night in the village, Kim and the lama set out
once again on their joint quest. On the villagers' advice they
walked southwards to join the Grand Trunk Road, because
this 'overpasses all the rivers of Hind', any one of which
might prove to be the lama's sacred stream. Moreover, it
would eventually carry them all the way to Benares, the
religious capital of India, where flows the holiest river of all,
the Ganges, and near which Buddha preached his first sermon, some 2,500 years ago. They were accompanied at first
by the old soldier, still bemused by Kim's prophecy of imminent war, who rode slowly along beside them. 'And now',
he announced proudly as they approached the slow-moving
lines of men, beasts and vehicles, 'we come to the Big Road
. . . the backbone of all Hind.'

# The Red Bull

The Grand Trunk Road, sometimes known as the Grand Military Road, or today as the GTR or NH1 – National Highway number 1 – dates back in parts to the Mogul era. But it was the British who exploited it as a means of maintaining control over their newly conquered territories, extending it north-westwards as they expanded into the Punjab and towards Afghanistan. Over the centuries of British rule the tree-lined highway felt the tramp of a hundred marching regiments and the rumble of heavy gun carriages as troops were moved up and down it from trouble-spot to trouble-spot. Along its 1,500-mile length were built garrison towns, transit camps, police stations and rest-houses in which travelling Raj officials could stay overnight. Hundreds, if not thousands, of bridges were built, embankments raised to lift the road above the flood-waters, and wells dug. Along it, in Kim's day, travelled the whole of India – 'such a river of life', wrote Kipling, 'as nowhere else exists in the world'.

Today it has changed, though not that much. Although some stretches have been turned into four-lane highways, with crash-barriers dividing the careering traffic, other parts are little wider than in Kim's day. On the busiest sectors it is choked with buses, trucks, taxis, country carts, herds of goats, men and women bearing huge loads, camels, elephants, motorised rickshaws and jingling tongas, all jockeying for position, while cyclists and motor-cyclists swerve in and out of this slow-moving concourse, sometimes vanishing completely in a giant puff of vulcan bus exhaust. It has been calculated that a bullock-cart, the slowest of all the road's many forms of transport, could take up to six months to travel its immense length, from Calcutta to the Khyber Pass. But not on all stretches does traffic move at a snail's pace, for some have been turned into virtual racetracks by truck-drivers who charge flat-out down the middle of the road, forcing other drivers mercilessly on to the treacherous verge, where many end up in the ditch. John Keay, who has written extensively on India, tells of one enraged Indian driver he once travelled with who armed himself with a revolver which he would brandish menacingly out of the window whenever he saw one of these monsters approaching, firing at their tyres if they refused to pull over. Usually, however, the sight of the pistol aimed straight at them was enough.

Yet today's murderous drivers are nothing compared to the nightmare which overtook much of the Grand Trunk Road during Partition, when entire villages were on the move trying to escape annihilation. In a few short weeks it was transformed from one of the safest and most peaceful roads on earth into perhaps the bloodiest thoroughfare in history. It was the same hideous story as that which took place on the trains, though today, as with the railway, it is hard for a traveller driving along the Grand Trunk Road to believe the things which once happened there. Louis Heren of *The Times* has described the desolation of the surrounding countryside as he drove along it in the summer of 1947: 'I had the impression that it had been visited by vast swarms of locusts.' Half blinded by tears, this toughest of reporters stood beside a well stuffed with slaughtered Muslims, includ-ing mothers with babies. 'I had never before seen anything so horrible,' he recalled in his memoirs.

Then, in the distance, he saw an enormous cloud of dust approaching from the direction of Pakistan. 'The cloud grew', he wrote, 'until it seemed to fill the western sky.' Soon, from its midst, emerged the first of more than a hundred bullock-carts, moving nose to tail, each filled with women and children and precious family possessions. On the soft shoulder, either side of the road, strode hundreds of men and boys, each with a headcloth over his face to keep out the choking dust. 'They looked like apparitions moving through one of those London fogs in Hollywood movies,' wrote Heren. 'The feeling of ghostliness was enhanced because they plodded past unseeing, and silently except for the squeaking cart axles. It was as if I did not exist . . .' Sadly, as I write this, I have just learned of the death of Heren, a colleague of mine on *The Times* for fifteen years, who had joined the paper in 1933, when I was only two. With his passing has been lost one of that fast-diminishing band of eye-witnesses to those dreadful events which so shamed the final days of British rule in India.

But let us return to Kim and the lama on the Grand Trunk Road in happier times, as they plunge into the confusion of men and beasts – 'all the world going and coming'. No words of mine can begin to do justice to Kipling's extraordinarily evocative account of life at that time on this great highway. It is a picture that few who have read *Kim*, no matter how long ago, ever forget. For it leaves in the reader's mind an indelible, near idyllic portrait of India. Even those critics who dislike just about everything that Kipling stood for (or is accused of standing for) grudgingly concede that it is one of the finest pieces of descriptive writing in the English language. 'A love letter to India', one has called it. Angus Wilson, Kipling's literary biographer, detects in it echoes of Chaucer's *Canterbury Tales* and also, to a lesser extent, Bunyan's *Pilgrim's Progress*, both known favourites of Kipling's. But he cites 'these impinging masterpieces of the past', he says, not because there is anything derivative about *Kim*, 'but rather to suggest the sort of literary heights in which we are travelling' in this work of 'absolute originality'.

Kim fell into step at the lama's side – 'that indescribable gait of the long-distance tramp all the world over', Kipling calls it. They walked together in silence thus for mile after mile, the old man clicking his prayer-beads and meditating, while Kim, in seventh heaven, gazed in fascination at the 'broad, smiling river of life' around him, with its many new people, castes and trades, and sights unknown to him in Lahore. Now and again, when they glimpsed water to left or right, they would turn momentarily off the busy highway to examine it. But from none of these muddy rivulets did the disappointed lama receive the mystic signs by which he would know instantly that this was the River of the Arrow.

However, there is much more to Kim and the lama's journey along the Grand Trunk Road than simply a piece of virtuoso writing by Kipling. Not only does it dramatically advance the narrative, it also introduces an important new member of the cast, this time a woman. As evening approached and weariness began to overcome them, Kim and the lama halted for the night at a crowded *parao*, or roadside resting place, where a row of simple shops sold basic necessities, among them food and firewood. With its constant comings and goings, its atmosphere reminded Kim of the Kashmir Serai by Lahore railway station. Just then, there drew into the *parao* close behind them a large bullock-cart with a brightly coloured canopy concealing its occupant. It

was escorted by eight men, two armed, and Kim realised at once that it contained someone of importance. Then, from behind the embroidered curtain, came the sharp, authoritative voice of a woman, clearly that of one used to issuing orders. Intrigued, Kim began to build their camp-fire as close as possible to where the mysterious new arrival and her retinue had now halted for the night.

For what happened next one must turn to *Kim* itself, so beautifully and comically is it told. Here it is sufficient to say that the invisible occupant turns out to be the wealthy and virtuous widow of a hill Raja, who now lives with her daughter at Saharunpore. Possessing a lively interest in religion, with a leaning towards Buddhism, she is currently on a pilgrimage to Buddh Gaya (now known as Bodhgaya), beyond Benares, where the Lord Buddha attained enlightenment. Following some spirited exchanges of wit with Kim from behind her canopy, she is captivated by his impudence and extravagant flattery, and at the same time is drawn to the lama, whose saintliness and simplicity touch her kindly heart. Kipling paints such a vivid and sympathetic portrait of her that it is hard to believe that he did not encounter such a woman on his travels. But whatever the truth, Kim and the lama were to form an abiding friendship with the formidable widow from Saharunpore – or the Sahiba, as Kipling calls her.

Having given them food from her kitchen, and quilts to sleep on, the Sahiba invites them next day to accompany her party to Buddh Gaya, so that she may continue to enjoy Kim's amusing repartee and the wisdom and spirituality of the lama. As this is the road they are taking anyway, they accept gratefully, and they all set out slowly southwards along the Grand Trunk Road. That evening they halt at another *parao*, from where Kim and the lama take a stroll while a meal is prepared. It is at this point that something occurs which is to change Kim's hitherto easy-going life by fulfilling the 'destiny' foretold by his father and confirmed by the priest at Umballa. For advancing across the plain towards them are four British soldiers, two of whom then halt. The other two, each carrying a long stick bearing a flag, continue. When quite close to Kim and the lama they stop, thrusting the sticks into the ground and allowing the flags to fly free. 'O Holy One! My horoscope!' cried Kim. For on each of the fluttering flags was the battalion insignia, a Red Bull on a green field. It was precisely as had been forecast. First would come two men to make all things ready. Indeed, it had come about on the very day that the priest had prophesied it would. He had also seen in Kim's stars war and hundreds of soldiers, and now, before their eyes, a long column of troops swung into view in the distance, marching to the sound of a regimental band. Halting, they immediately began pitching tents in the area marked out by the men with flags.

Having seen all he wanted for the moment, Kim led the bemused lama, who had never witnessed anything like this before, back to the Sahiba's little camp. But later that evening Kim again slipped out, bent on discovering more about his Red Bull. Sneaking past the sentries, he crept towards the largest and most brightly lit of the many tents. This, though he did not know it, served as the officers' mess. The regiment, of course, was that of his father, Kipling's mythical Mavericks – which explains the 'nine hundred first-class devils' in his prophecy, that being the strength of a serving battalion. Inside the tent Kim saw a long table surrounded by sahibs in uniform. In the middle of the table, astride a piece of Irish green baize, stood an impressive red-gold sculpture of a bull, 'liberated', as it happened, from the Summer Palace in Peking, and now the pride of the regiment's silver. The sahibs appeared to Kim to be praying to the bull, for they extended their glasses towards it, muttering something incomprehensible as they did so. But that was the last that Kim saw of the curious goings-on in the tent, for at that moment the Reverend Arthur Bennett, the Mavericks' Protestant chaplain, emerged unexpectedly from inside and tripped headlong over the recumbent spy.

Things now began to happen fast. Assuming Kim to be a thief, Bennett dragged him into his tent, at the same time calling to his Catholic colleague, Father Victor. Together they began to interrogate the protesting Kim, who insisted that he was no thief but the *chela* to a very holy man, and that he was merely pursuing a prophecy about a Red Bull which had been fulfilled that very day. It was only when they noticed that Kim spoke English and that beneath his ragged shirt his skin was white, and when they had examined the papers in his amulet-case, that the astonished chaplains realised who he really was – the son of Colour-Sergeant Kimball O'Hara, late of the Mavericks. Now the painful problem arose of what to do with this regimental orphan, for his dying father had scrawled repeatedly on one of the papers: '*Look after the boy. Please look after the boy.*' The most obvious solution, the two chaplains agreed, would be for Kim to be sent to an orphanage, either a military one or a Masonic one, his father having been a member of the regimental lodge. Kim, who has narrowly avoided being sent to such institutions all his life, objects strongly to this suggestion, demanding angrily that he be freed at once so that he can return to his holy man, who is waiting anxiously for him somewhere outside.

## The Red Bull

At this point the lama is found and brought in, and using Kim as the interpreter the chaplains explain the situation to him. There now follow some of the most poignant moments in the entire book, as the old man realises that he is about to lose the *chela* he has grown to love like a son and also depend on to pilot him through the shoals of 'this great and terrible world'. Kim has to break it to him that he has deceived him from the start, and that he is really a sahib. But the lama immediately blames himself for everything. 'The sin is mine and the punishment is mine,' he declares bitterly. 'I made believe to myself – for now I see it was but make-belief – that thou was sent to me to aid in the Search. So my heart went out to thee for thy charity and thy courtesy and the wisdom of thy little years.' The River of the Arrow was now as far away as ever, he added, because he had broken 'the Law' and had become attached to another human being. Father Victor – 'wise in the confessional', Kipling tells us – 'heard the pain in every sentence'. But so sensitively and movingly is this passage told that it must be read in the original.

The lama insists on knowing what the white men plan to do with his disciple, and is deeply troubled to learn that he will probably be trained as a soldier, like his father. Kim, too, is horrified, for the prospect of 'drill and routine' is anathema to him. On further questioning, though, the lama learns that 'wise and suitable teaching' could be obtained for Kim at a very good school – 'the best schooling a boy can get in India', Father Victor assures him – at Lucknow, but that this would cost between two and three hundred rupees a year. To the chaplain's astonishment, the lama asks for the name of the school – St Xavier in Partibus – to be written down for him. He then disappears into the night, but not before the distraught Kim, who has become greatly attached to the old man, has whispered to him that he should travel on to Benares with the kindly Sahiba's party. In this way he will be able to find the lama and rejoin him as soon as he can escape the clutches of the sahibs.

By now other officers, including the Mavericks' colonel, have been brought in, and Kim is questioned at length. He amuses everyone by announcing that the regiment will very shortly be going to war. Such amusement turns to astonishment when orders arrive next day for the Mavericks to entrain at Umballa for a campaign somewhere in the far north. Meanwhile, dressed in a scratchy, uncomfortable uniform, Kim finds himself incarcerated in the barracks at Umballa and made to attend lessons with the regimental drummer-boys, who mock and bully him mercilessly. The plan is, unless the lama comes up with the St Xavier school fees, to send him to a military orphanage at Sanawar, the Mavericks' depot in the Simla hills, where there was, in fact, a school for the orphans of British soldiers in Kipling's day.

Desperate to escape, Kim sends a despairing message to his old friend Mahbub Ali via a letter-writer, telling him what has happened and begging him to come and rescue him. The Afghan horse-dealer moves swiftly, arriving in Umballa four days later. He snatches Kim up on to his saddle and gallops off with him to the Umballa racecourse where he knows that Colonel Creighton will be exercising his horse.

He then proceeds to 'sell' Kim to the secret service chief, explaining that he was the young beggar who delivered the vital papers to the bungalow, and impressing on the Englishman that Kim is ideal material for the Great Game. Disguising his words in the language of the horse-trade, lest they be overheard, he tells Creighton: 'I have some young stuff coming on made by Heaven for the delicate and difficult polo-game.' This pony, he adds, indicating the uncomprehending Kim, 'has no equal'. He argues, moreover, that if Kim is sent to a military orphanage he will quickly lose his unique bent for intelligence work, resulting from his extraordinary background. 'They will send him to school and put heavy boots on his feet,' the Afghan warns. 'Then he will forget all he knows.'

As it happens, as though by a miracle, Father Victor receives that very day a 'native note of hand' for Kim's St Xavier school fees for a whole year, with a promise from the lama that the subsequent years' fees will also be paid. For by now the old man has reached Benares safely, and is staying with friends at a temple belonging to the Tirthankars, or Jains. Founded by Buddha's own son, the faith of the Jains is closely related to Buddhism in many of its beliefs, particularly with regard to all living creatures – so much so, in fact, that some Jains cover their mouths lest they accidentally inhale flying insects, and brush the ground before them to avoid treading on any creature. Just how the lama has come by this money, and so swiftly, Kipling does not attempt to explain. But it is no secret that some monasteries in Tibet were very rich, their treasuries filled with the offerings of the devout (or extorted, the Communists would claim, from the superstitious local peasantry). All that Kipling does tell us is that the money arrived via one Gobind Sahai, a native banker, whose notes of hand, Creighton declares, 'are good from here to China'. Perhaps, pending its arrival across the Himalayan passes, Gobind advanced the money, knowing of the wealth of the lama's monastery by repute, or perhaps the Tirthankars loaned it to the lama, so anxious was he that his beloved *chela* should be saved from becoming a soldier, and instead devote his life to learning, like the kindly Keeper of Images at Lahore. One can only speculate.

Welcoming this astonishing and unexpected munificence, the colonel strongly urged that the Tibetan's offer be taken up, and Kim be sent to St Xavier's in Lucknow. For he knew that there the boy would be taught elementary surveying and other skills invaluable to the career he foresaw for this brilliant young colt, so clearly 'born to be a polo-pony'. Before cantering off, Mahbub Ali whispers to an agonised Kim: 'Thy fortune is made ... I shall see thee again, I think, many times.' Creighton then addresses Kim in Urdu. 'Listen to me. In three days thou wilt go with me to Lucknow, seeing and hearing new things all the while. Therefore sit still and do not run away.' Mahbub Ali, he warned, would be very angry 'if thou returnest to the Road now'.

On leaving the colonel, the first thing that Kim did was to hasten to the letter-writer who had penned his plea to Mahbub Ali, and send an urgent message to the lama, the only adult he really trusted, warning him that he would shortly be on his way to Lucknow to begin his schooling.

## The Red Bull

Three days later he found himself seated alone in a second-class railway compartment next to Colonel Creighton's first-class one, heading southwards to 'Nucklao', as Kim called it, and 'to he knew not what fate'. But the reader knows, if Kim does not, that his initiation into the secrets of the Great Game is about to begin.

# 7

# *Who Was Colonel Creighton?*

ONE OF THE great joys of *Kim* is that the characters are forever on the move, with endless comings and goings, whether by 'te-rain', bullock-cart or on foot. There are few static moments, and these are usually short-lived. Whenever the story moves on, the sheer size of the country means a long journey – from Lahore to Umballa, Umballa to Lucknow, Lucknow to Simla, and so on. For years I had wondered why Kipling chose Lucknow – more than 500 miles from Lahore – as the site of St Xavier's, since it appeared so distant from those parts of India with which he is usually associated. Others must have wondered too, for one modern guidebook which should know better informs us, quite wrongly, that Kipling himself went to this same school for several years.

I was aware that Kipling spent the final two of his 'Seven Years' Hard', as he describes his time in India, working for the *Pioneer* in Allahabad. But because of this city's Islamic-sounding name I had rather stupidly assumed that it must lie in some out-of-the-way corner of Pakistan which I must have missed on my earlier travels. It was only when I pored over maps of *Kim* country when planning this journey that it all suddenly became clear. For despite its name, Allahabad lies squarely in India. And close by, making a neat triangle, are Lucknow and Benares. The latter cities would therefore have been familiar to Kipling, for they lay within the area from which the *Pioneer* gathered its news.

The owners of the *Pioneer* allowed the young Kipling a good deal more freedom to write about what he chose than he had enjoyed on the *Civil and Military Gazette* in Lahore. This enabled him to evolve his very distinctive and original style of writing which we see at its consummate best in the pages of *Kim*. 'I made my own experiments', he wrote years afterwards, 'in the weights, colours, perfumes, and attributes of words in relation to other words, either as read aloud so that they may hold the ear, or, scattered over the page, draw the eye. There is no line of my verse or prose which has not been mouthed till the tongue has made all smooth . . .' One clever literary device which he made his own, and which he exploits to the full in *Kim*, is the use of capital letters to heighten the impact of a name or phrase. Thus we get the Great Game (earlier writers had always written it with a small g), the Wonder House, the Red Bull, the River of the Arrow, the Northern Power, the Five Kings, the Passes of the North, the Hills, the Road, Little Friend of all the World, the Way, Holy One – and so on, oft-repeated, throughout the book. These, 'scattered over the page', certainly draw the eye, as well as adding an air of mystery or romance to the narrative.

Yet another of Kipling's highly effective tricks for creating atmosphere is his use of vernacular dialogue, or at least what sounds like it, which he translates into English for us. This gives us sentences like: 'If thou wilt carry a message for me as far as Umballa, I will give thee money', and 'Never have I seen such a man as thou art.' Such dialogue is usually reserved for Kim, who is all but a native, and the book's non-European characters. However, even a pukka English-man like Colonel Creighton can be made to speak like this, as we see as he and Kim travel down to Lucknow together (a journey which, we learn, then took twenty-four hours, but today takes only twelve). It is during this train ride that Creighton calls Kim into his first-class compartment to tell him a little of what is in store for him. At first he addresses him in English, but Kim, playing along with the role which he knows is desired of him by Creighton and Mahbub Ali, pretends to understand 'perhaps one word in three of this talk'. Creighton, 'seeing his mistake', then switches to 'fluent and picturesque Urdu', thereby enabling Kipling to employ his vernacular translation device.

Having told Kim that he will be taught the art of surveying at St Xavier's, Creighton continues: 'Yes, and thou must learn how to make pictures of roads and mountains and rivers – to carry these pictures in thine eyes till a suitable time comes to set them down upon paper.' He also warns Kim that he may be sent on dangerous missions beyond the hills where 'bad people' dwell who will kill him if they discover that he is really a sahib, and that he may be required to bring back 'news of what people say in the villages there'. These are the first intimations that Kim receives of how Creighton and Mahbub Ali eventually intend to use his chameleon-like qualities. Officially, however, when he leaves St Xavier's he will join the Survey of India as a 'chain man', named after the jointed iron measuring rod then used by surveyors, earning seventeen rupees a month.

All this brings us back to the intriguing question of whom Kipling had in mind when he created the shadowy character of Colonel Creighton, head of the British intelligence service in India. For the clues are now beginning to point in one direction only, and anyone who has read either my *Trespassers on the Roof of the World* or *The Great Game* will almost certainly have guessed who my candidate is. Kim, it is clear from Creighton's briefing, is to be trained as a 'pundit', that élite band of Indian explorers employed by the British to gather topographical and other intelligence in areas where it was too dangerous for Europeans to travel. These men, who were really spies, were the brain-child of a certain Colonel (then Captain) Thomas Montgomerie of the Survey of India. An officer of great ingenuity, he trained these hand-picked individuals in clandestine surveying techniques devised by himself which would permit them to work undercover beyond the frontiers of British India, thus enabling the Survey to produce maps of the strategic approaches which an invader might use.

Montgomerie first taught his men, through exhaustive practice, to take a pace of known length which would remain constant whether walking uphill, downhill or on the level. Next he devised furtive ways whereby they could keep a precise but discreet count of the number of such measured

paces taken during a long day's march. Some travelled as Buddhist pilgrims, with rosaries and prayer-wheels, which Montgomerie's workshops at Dehra Dun, the Survey's headquarters, cunningly doctored for clandestine use. Buddhist rosaries, like that carried by the lama, normally consist of 108 beads, a sacred number, which enables the owner to keep a tally of his prayers. Simply by removing eight of these, not enough to be noticed, one is left with a mathematically convenient 100. At every hundredth pace the bogus pilgrim would automatically slip one bead, enabling him to clock up 10,000 such measured strides with each complete circuit of the rosary. But at the end of every day, or at some other convenient moment, the clandestine surveyor had to log the distance he had covered, together with any other discreet observations, in a place secure from prying eyes. It was here that the Buddhist prayer-wheel, with its copper cylinder, proved invaluable. For hidden in this, instead of the usual scroll of prayers, was a roll of blank paper. This served Montgomerie's spies as a secret log book, which could easily be got at by removing the top of the cylinder. At the same time a small compass was concealed in the cylinder lid itself, while thermometers, required for calculating altitudes, were hidden in the tops of pilgrims' staves. These were merely some of the ingenious devices dreamed up by the remarkable Montgomerie for use by the men he dispatched into Afghanistan, Turkestan and Tibet, the story of whom I have told in considerable detail elsewhere. All I hope to do here is to convince the reader that Colonel Montgomerie is the most likely model for Creighton, there being no other serious contender, at least not in my mind. One or two other names have been suggested in the past, though none very convincingly.

Although the activities and methods of the 'pundits', who operated during the 1860s, '70s and early '80s, were supposedly secret, a number of accounts of their journeys were published in the Royal Geographical Society's *Journal*, albeit without identifying them beyond their code-names, lest they be put at risk in future operations. Kipling, who was remarkably well read, and who also had the benefit of his father's profound knowledge of Indian affairs, certainly knew about them and their exotic *modus operandi*. It seems fairly obvious, to begin with, that he borrowed the idea of code-names – C25, R17 and E23 – from Montgomerie, as well as the use of disguise, which crops up frequently in *Kim*. In addition, as we shall see in due course, Kim is to receive a thoroughgoing pundit-style training (plus certain colourful embellishments devised by Kipling) under the personal direction of Colonel Creighton, with Mahbub Ali and other veterans of the game lending a hand.

If Kipling knew so much about the 'pundits', then it seems highly unlikely that he would not have known about their legendary creator. Certainly the two would never have met, for Montgomerie died aged only forty-seven, his health broken, when Kipling was still a schoolboy. Of course, Montgomerie was never head of the Indian secret service, for there was no such organisation at that time. However, the clandestine side of the Survey of India, with Colonel Montgomerie as its mastermind, was then the nearest thing to it. Seizing on Montgomerie's brilliant concept, Kipling simply extended it into an India-wide intelligence service, using the (Kipling-invented) 'Ethnographical Department' of the (real-life) Survey of India as its front organisation.

Kipling rarely drew his characters simply from one person – or so Kipling scholars will tell you. However, in the case of Creighton there is a strong case for arguing that he was inspired by Montgomerie alone. For a start, we are told very little about Creighton, not even what he looks like, although his influence is strongly felt throughout the rest of the book.

## Who Was Colonel Creighton?

The emphasis is on the peculiar nature of his work, and his novel means of pursuing it, rather than on his person. Thus there are no obvious signs of anyone other than Montgomerie in him – or not that I can detect. Indeed, one would be hard-pressed to improve on the real-life genius who dreamed up the 'pundits' and their bizarre paraphernalia of tricks. Nevertheless, in his contribution to *The Reader's Guide to Rudyard Kipling's Works*, published in 1961, Brigadier Alec Mason suggests that his uncle, Lieutenant-Colonel A.H. Mason, CB, DSO, was the model for Creighton. Unfortunately he provides no evidence or explanation to support his claim, and because both he and his uncle are dead this somewhat vague theory cannot be pursued further. Certainly Colonel Mason, who died in 1896, is not to be found in the authoritative *Dictionary of Indian Biography*, which was published in 1906 and which outlines the careers of 2,600 individuals, including Colonel Montgomerie, whose covert activities are described.

Although in Kim's day, and for a long time afterwards, there was no Indian secret service of the all-seeing kind so vividly portrayed by Kipling, the Tsarist advance across Central Asia towards India did cause much loss of sleep among the British military hierarchy at Simla. In 1879, therefore, they set up a small department consisting of five officers, two of them only part-time, and two Indian clerks, calling itself the Intelligence Branch. Its function was to gather, by more or less conventional means, data on Russian troop dispositions in Central Asia, and Russian military maps of the area, and to translate any relevant military literature into

English. All non-military intelligence – particularly on matters such as the current dependability of certain maharajas and tribal rulers – was the jealous preserve of the Foreign and Political Department, the nearest thing India had to its own Foreign Office, with representatives at the courts of the Indian princes and even in the Persian Gulf states. Both these intelligence-gathering bodies, however, were a far cry from the shadowy organisation employing Afghan horse-dealers, and even stranger individuals whom we have yet to meet, invented by Kipling.

Curiously enough, Kipling showed remarkable prescience in inventing this organisation. For in 1904, three years after *Kim* was published, an intelligence service was set up which closely resembled Creighton's all-seeing, all-India spy network. Fears of nationalist sedition, possibly directed from abroad, had long haunted the handful of expatriate British officials who controlled the lives and destinies of one-fifth of the entire human race. But this now suddenly became a frightening reality as a campaign of bombings, assassinations and other acts of anti-Raj terrorism threatened to tear India apart. In the winter of 1907, two attempts were made to blow up the official train of the Lieutenant-Governor of Bengal, while two years later the Viceroy himself had a narrow escape when two bombs tossed at his open carriage both fell short. Other attempts on the lives of senior Raj officials followed, some of them successful, while lesser figures, many of them Indians in British employ, fell victim to assassins' bullets and bombs at a rate of one a fortnight. In 1912, the then Viceroy Lord Hardinge was very nearly killed when a

bomb was thrown at him as he and his wife rode ceremoniously into Delhi, India's new capital, on the back of an
elephant. The Viceroy was injured in the explosion, which
was heard six miles away, but the would-be assassin escaped
into the crowd.

The man entrusted with the task of destroying this 'enemy
within' was Sir Charles Cleveland, Director of Criminal
Intelligence, also known as Central Intelligence. A man of
herculean strength, he had played Rugby football for both
Oxford and England, and had once swung a wounded pan-
ther, which was clinging to his arm, round and round until
it could be clubbed to death by his bearer. But Cleveland
was not all brawn. A Balliol man, he also possessed a first-class
brain which he pitted against those of the conspirators with
considerable success, dispatching scores of convicted
bombers, assassins and other terrorists and seditionists to the
gallows. 'His flair was amazing,' a former colleague recalled,
and his genius for outwitting the conspirators 'almost
uncanny'. I have described some of his greatest successes
against German-backed terrorists in the First World War in
*On Secret Service East of Constantinople.* Had he been
operating a quarter of a century earlier, one would have
had to consider him a possible rival to Montgomerie as the
inspiration for Kipling's mysterious Creighton. In the event,
he only took up his appointment of what was, effectively,
the Indian secret service some twenty years after Kipling had
left the country for good.

But our exploration of Creighton's possible origins has
carried us a long way from where we left him and his appre-

hensive young protégé as they travelled down to Lucknow by train together. During his long hours by himself in his second-class compartment, Kim had had much time for reflection over this dramatic change in his fortunes. For the first time in his young life he asked himself: 'Who is Kim?' Until his chance meeting with the lama outside the Lahore museum, he had simply been a carefree street-child who lived by his wits and rarely questioned anything. Now, almost overnight, he had begun to grow up. In the saintly lama he had found a surrogate father, or perhaps grandfather, for his own parents were only a dim memory. At first he had looked upon this strange figure as a sort of collector's piece, something he could show off. But gradually this had changed, and he found himself becoming increasingly attached to this gentle, selfless man of almost unbelievable innocence who had saved him from imprisonment in an orphanage by paying his school fees. The transformation of Kim from a feckless, bazaar-educated urchin to a serious and thoughtful youngster is one of the book's most memorable and enduring themes.

Having eagerly written ahead to the lama to alert him to his coming, Kim was disappointed not to find him waiting at Lucknow railway station. Instead, he was unceremoniously bundled into a tonga by Creighton with instructions to proceed straight to St Xavier's. But anxious to enjoy his last moments of freedom, Kim ordered the driver to take him on a tour of the city in which he knew he would be spending most of the next three years. Only then did he ask the driver to head for St Xavier's, which lay on the outskirts of the town, on a bend of the River Gomti, or Gumti as the British call it. It was there, as they approached the school's great wrought-iron gates, that Kim's keen eyes spotted a familiar, yellow-robed figure in the shadow of a wall. To his intense joy, he recognised the lama. On receiving Kim's letter, the old man had at once caught the 'te-rain' up from Benares, where he was staying at the Jain temple while continuing his search for his sacred river. He had, it transpired, been waiting outside St Xavier's for a day and a half, hoping to see Kim before he entered this school for young sahibs, which would turn him into a scholar like the Keeper of Images at Lahore.

Kim leaped down from the tonga and threw himself at the Tibetan's feet, making no attempt to conceal his happiness at this reunion. But the lama, struggling to contain his own emotions at seeing his *chela*, hastily assured Kim that it was not any fondness for him that had brought him hurrying from Benares. It was, he insisted, simply so that he could oversee his entry into St Xavier's. 'I had a fear', he admitted, 'that, perhaps, I came because I wished to see thee – misguided by the Red Mist of affection.' To this he added quickly, if unconvincingly: 'It is not so . . .' Crestfallen, Kim asked him tearfully: 'Surely it was a little to see me that thou didst come?' But the lama was insistent. Brushing aside the boy's pleas for him to stay, he told him: 'No – no. I must go back to Benares. From time to time, now that I know the customs of letter-writers in this land, I will send thee a letter, and from time to time I will come and see thee. Do not weep . . . all Desire is Illusion and a new binding upon the Wheel.'

Now came the painful moment of parting. In describing it, Kipling must have recalled his own traumatic separation from his parents at the age of six, when they left him in England to return to India, which was to scar him for life. The lama, his voice quavering, ordered Kim to drive in through the school gates. 'I will come again. Surely I will come again,' he promised, before watching the tonga disappear into the courtyard of St Xavier's. Then, hurriedly taking some snuff to hide his own distress, he strode off towards the railway station. Behind him, wrote Kipling, 'the Gates of Learning shut with a clang'.

# 8

# School for Spies

THERE IS, of course, no such school in Lucknow as St Xavier in Partibus, and there never was – at least not under that name. But, like almost everything else in *Kim*, the school which was to transform this ragged and illiterate street urchin into a young football-playing sahib was far from being a total Kipling invention. Few, if any, Kipling scholars doubt that St Xavier's was modelled on one of the most renowned public schools in British India – the remarkable La Martinière College – which just happens to be in Lucknow. Like St Xavier's, moreover, La Martinière 'stands in vast grounds over against the Gumti River, at some distance from the city'. For good measure, it is the only large boarding school for boys in Lucknow dating back to Kipling's day. Finally, old boys I have spoken to who were there either during the last days of the Raj or subsequently all unfailingly recognise La Martinière in the pages of *Kim*.

*School for Spies*

The story of La Martinière itself is almost as strange as anything out of *Kim*, and would certainly have appealed to Kipling's imagination. Housed in a vast and impressive building – a sort of cross between the Victoria and Albert Museum and the Albert Hall – it was originally built as his residence by a French adventurer named Claude Martin, who rose to the rank of general in the East India Company's army. He also became a millionaire. On his death, in 1800, he left a large sum of money for the endowment of a boys' school to be named La Martinière, after himself. Every year, on the anniversary of his death, a sermon was to be preached to the boys, which was to be followed by a dinner at which a toast was to be drunk to his memory. He also left a large sum of money to be distributed daily, in perpetuity, to the poor of Lucknow and Calcutta at certain fixed points distinguished by tablets bearing inscriptions in English, French and Persian.

Rather more bizarrely, he instructed in his will 'that my body be salted, put in spirits, or embalmed', and placed in a lead coffin in a vault beneath the school. His tomb, he requested, should carry a plaque bearing the following inscription:

Major-General Claude Martin.
Arrived in India as a common soldier, and died at Lucknow on the 13th of September, 1800, as a Major-General. He is buried in this tomb. Pray for his soul.

Something more than pure vanity lay behind all this, however. Martin was aware that the Nawab, the Muslim ruler of the independent kingdom in which Lucknow then lay, coveted this grand residence, and would try to obtain it after his death. By having himself, a Christian, buried beneath it, he knew that he would effectively and permanently desecrate it in the Nawab's eyes. When, thirty years later, Lady Fanny Parkes visited his subterranean tomb, she noted that a bust of Martin adorned the vault, lights burned continually before it, and the sculptured, life-size figures of four soldiers, their weapons reversed, watched over it from niches in the wall.

Quite apart from all this, the building itself possessed some unique features introduced by Martin, including special living quarters designed to lessen the discomforts of Lucknow's disagreeable climate. In the height of summer, when temperatures become unbearable, Martin would move down into a large underground suite, where it was considerably cooler. During the monsoon, when the entire ground floor would sometimes be flooded by the overflowing Gumti, he would ascend to the upper storey, taking his furniture and valuables with him.

However, that is not all that is remarkable about La Martinière. During the Indian Mutiny, when Lucknow was besieged by rebel forces, the school was evacuated and the senior boys fought shoulder to shoulder with the defenders of the beleaguered British Residency, while the younger ones, often under heavy fire, carried ammunition and food to them, and assisted in the makeshift hospital. Eventually, after a defence lasting five months, a British relief party fought its way through to Lucknow, enabling the hard-pressed garrison to be evacuated. The now ragged La Martinière boys made their way, under a military escort, first to Allahabad and then to Benares, a perilous journey which took them a month and a half. In Benares the school was found a temporary home, only returning to its own damaged building in Lucknow after an absence of nearly two years.

In recognition of their courage and steadfastness, each boy was awarded the Indian Mutiny Medal, with the words 'Defence of Lucknow' inscribed on it. As a further honour, La Martinière was also granted the right, on ceremonial occasions, to carry a British Army regimental-style colour bearing its own coat of arms with the words 'Defence of Lucknow, 1857' beneath an embroidered portrait of the Residency. It thus became the only school in the British Empire to possess a battle-honour. One of the senior boys – Edward Hilton, who was seventeen at the time, and who was wounded in the fighting – left a detailed account of the siege. He tells us that on their return to the school they found that the rebels had destroyed General Martin's tomb, including the commemorative plaque and bust and the four life-size figures of soldiers. They had also scattered his bones, though these were subsequently recovered and respectfully restored to their original resting place beneath the building's central tower. Some years later, when renovation work was being carried out in the school grounds, large quantities of spent bullets, cannon balls and other rusting weaponry were brought to light, showing the ferocity of the fighting. Such then, albeit under another name, was the extraordinary school to which Kipling chose to send Kim.

Some of the St Xavier boys, Kim soon discovered from dormitory tales exchanged during the long, stifling Lucknow nights, lived lives hardly less adventurous than those of the La Martinière heroes. Their parents were mostly Anglo-Indian officials ('half-sahibs', Mahbub Ali dubbed them) of the railway, canal and telegraph services, or missionaries, planters or merchant navy captains, while some – former British warrant-officers – served as commanders-in-chief to the armies of petty rajahs. They came, Kipling tells us, from far and wide – from mission-stations a week from the nearest railway, from remote tea-gardens lost in the jungle, and from seaports a thousand miles to the south. For some, simply getting to school each term could be hazardous enough. 'The mere story of their adventures, which to them were no adventures,' wrote Kipling, 'would have crisped a Western boy's hair. They were used to jogging off alone through a hundred miles of jungle . . . but they would no more have bathed in the English Channel in an English August than their brothers across the world would have lain still while a leopard snuffed at their palanquin.' There were boys of fifteen 'who had spent a day and a half on an islet in the middle of a flooded river, taking charge, as by right, of a camp of frantic pilgrims', while another said – 'and none doubted' – that he had helped his father beat off an attack by head-hunters on their isolated plantation.

Before travelling out to Pakistan and India to retrace Kim's footsteps, I had written to the headmaster of La Martinière, hoping to discover more about this school on which Kipling had modelled St Xavier's. Most of all, I wanted to know whether the present generation of staff and boys were even aware of the connection. But either the Indian postal service swallowed up my letter or his reply, or perhaps he felt he had better things to do than answer idle questions about a fictitious school celebrated only in imperialist literature. Whatever the reason, I never heard from him. But then I had a sudden stroke of luck. A friend of mine, hearing that I was writing a book about *Kim*, mentioned that he knew someone who had actually been at La Martinière during the last days of the Raj. Now in his mid-sixties and living in Cambridge, this former La Martinière pupil said he would be delighted to talk to me about the school as he remembered it nearly half a century ago. The story that emerged proved every bit as harrowing and extraordinary as any of those told in the dormitory at St Xavier's.

Stephen Brookes, the son of a retired British Army doctor and his young Burmese wife, still has nightmares, more than fifty years afterwards, about the journey which eventually led him to La Martinière. In April 1942, when he was only eleven, the Japanese invaded Burma, where he was then living with his parents and his older brother and sister. They had tried, in vain, to leave on one of the last two aircraft to ferry out refugees. Stephen had somehow got ahead of the other four on the steps leading up to one of the aircraft when they shouted to him to come back down. For they could see that there would not be room on the overcrowded plane for all five of them. It was to prove a miraculous escape, for both aircraft were shot down by the Japanese shortly after take-off, with the loss of everyone on board.

But worse, far worse, was to follow. The only way now left to avoid imprisonment or death at the hands of the advancing Japanese was by fleeing on foot, through three hundred miles of mountain and jungle, to British India. Their journey, made in the company of thousands of other refugees also streaming westwards, was to take them six agonising months. Stephen is still haunted by the memory of stepping over hundreds of corpses as, ragged, hungry and exhausted, they struggled on. In addition to being bombed and machine-gunned by Japanese aircraft, they were regularly ambushed by lawless Chinese soldiery, supposedly their allies, who robbed them at gunpoint of the few possessions they had been able to carry with them.

On June 27, two months after setting out, they celebrated – if it can be called that – Stephen's twelfth birthday. Then, a month later, disaster struck. Already gravely weakened by the privations of the journey, Stephen's father, now seventy, died of blackwater fever, a rare form of malaria, while his family looked on helplessly. At times the others came close to death too. Stephen's sister, aged eighteen, was lucky to survive cerebral malaria, which is frequently fatal, while his brother, then thirteen, was reduced to a near skeleton by dysentery. Their mother, Stephen now realises, was on the verge of a nervous breakdown, so overburdened was she by grief and responsibility. Blessed with great resilience himself, Stephen had frequently to nurse the others through sickness and delirium.

Finally, in October 1942, they reached India – and safety. However, their immediate troubles were far from over, for they were totally destitute, and had no papers to prove who they were, or even that they were British citizens. Eventually, though, Stephen was found a place in a school, from where he won a scholarship to La Martinière. Despite his appalling experiences, not to mention six months without any schooling, he was to distinguish himself at La Martinière, both at work and as an athlete. The ten silver cups he won for middle- and long-distance running today grace his Cambridge living-room. Before we met there, Stephen had re-read *Kim*, particularly the part describing Kim's years at St Xavier's. It left him in no doubt that La Martinière and St Xavier's were one and the same. For little seemed to have changed between Kim's day and his, and the book brought back very happy memories of his own schooldays in Lucknow, although these would always be overshadowed by the nightmare of his escape from Burma.

The conviction that Kipling chose La Martinière as the model for St Xavier's did not die with the departure of the British and the Indianisation of the school. One Old Martinian, as its alumni now call themselves, who was there long after the end of the Raj, told me that everyone at the school, both boys and masters, was aware that it was the inspiration for St Xavier's. Today a senior executive with Oxford University Press in Delhi, and himself a novelist, Rukon Advani added: 'Even if there is no concrete or verbatim evidence to this effect, the view in Lucknow and elsewhere in India's educated circles is that the school in Kipling's novel is modelled on La Martinière.' Plenty of people all over India, he said, still read *Kim*. 'It is frequently a prescribed text at the BA Hons. level in many of our 140 or so universities.' He is planning, he told me, to commission a leading Indian scholar to write an introduction and notes to a new paperback reprint of *Kim*. Meanwhile both the Oxford University Press World Classics edition of the book, and the Penguin version, continue to sell very well in India.

But we must return to Kim, who by now was settling into public school life rather better than Colonel Creighton or Father Victor had ever dared hope, and was even getting used to wearing a young sahib's white drill suit. Unusually for him, moreover, he was learning to keep his mouth shut. He could easily have capped any of the other boys' dormitory tales with his own adventures on the rooftops and in the bazaars and alleyways of old Lahore, but he knew that St Xavier's looked down on boys who 'went native', so he kept quiet. For the one thing the school never allowed its pupils to forget was that first and foremost they were sahibs, and that one day, when their final examinations were over, it would be their imperial destiny to 'command natives'. Yet although Kim was enjoying most of the new experiences provided by St Xavier's, he sometimes yearned for his old carefree life, especially for the tasty but forbidden – to St Xavier's boys, that is – food of the bazaar, and 'for the caress of soft mud squishing up between the toes'.

It was to his dismay, therefore, that he learned that he was to spend the long Indian summer holidays, lasting from August to October, at an army barrack-school in a hill-station north of Umballa. This had been arranged by the well-meaning Father Victor, while Colonel Creighton had provided him with a rail warrant. Kim, who had studied diligently during the term, rebelled at the prospect of spending the next three months in this way. A boy's holiday, like an adult's, should be his own to do what he liked with, he decided. As the trunks were being packed for the holidays, he was careful to give no hint of these thoughts to anyone, but on the last day of term, instead of heading straight for the railway station like the other boys, Kim made his way to Lucknow's red-light district. Here, he knew from his Lahore days, he would find easy-going girls who would do his bidding without question, especially now that he was a young sahib. And so it proved, for half an hour later, after much tittering from within, Kim emerged. His entire skin had been darkened with a dye 'that holds longer than any walnut juice', his St Xavier-length hair had been shorn off and, with the help of some cheap material bought in the bazaar, he had been transformed into a low-caste Hindu boy, 'perfect in every detail'. Clutching Colonel Creighton's rail pass, he now made swiftly for the station where he caught the first train to Umballa.

Not long afterwards, on discovering Kim's trunk still in his dormitory, and no sign of him, the St Xavier's authorities immediately telegraphed Colonel Creighton to warn him that O'Hara had vanished. The secret service chief was greatly alarmed, fearing lest some misfortune had befallen his young protégé. He immediately consulted Mahbub Ali, who reassured him that he need not worry. 'He has gone back to the Road again for a while,' the Afghan told him. 'The *madrissah* wearied him. I knew it would.' He himself was not the least concerned about Kim's safety. 'A monkey', he added, 'does not fall among trees.' Kim, meanwhile, euphoric at being once again his own master, had left the train at Umballa, where his rail pass ran out, and had made his way across the fields to where he knew the old soldier, with whom he had stayed before, lived, and who he was sure would welcome him. While he was there he would decide just how he was going to spend his holidays.

Shortly after this Mahbub Ali, who was in Simla with Colonel Creighton, ostensibly delivering polo ponies, received a letter from Kim, who had somehow got wind of his presence there. In it Kim explained why he had rejected the barrack-school for 'the Road'. Choosing words that he knew Mahbub Ali – and hopefully Colonel Creighton – would understand, he declared: 'Certain things are not known to those who eat with forks.' It would be better, therefore, if he were 'to eat with both hands for a while'. Aware, however, that Creighton would be angry with him for his truancy, he begged his Afghan friend to 'let the Hand of Friendship turn aside the Whip of Calamity', or, put more simply, to intercede with the colonel on his behalf. Despite these protestations of penitence, his letter gave no clues as to his whereabouts, or how he was planning to spend his holidays, although he solemnly undertook to return to St Xavier's in time for the new term. Defending Kim, Mahbub Ali reminded Creighton: 'When he comes to the Great Game he must go alone – alone, and at peril of his head.

Then, if he spits, or sneezes, or sits down other than as the people do whom he watches, he may be slain.' Relieved to discover that his young protégé was still alive, the colonel relented, although he insisted that Kim should not venture off alone in future.

A month later, as Mahbub Ali was on his way down to Umballa to collect a fresh batch of ponies, he was accosted on the road in the dusk by a young beggar who demanded alms. Cursing the boy, he rode on, only to hear himself reproached in English. In a flash he realised that it was Kim. Together they sat beneath a tree and exchanged news. Kim, it transpired, had visited Delhi – 'a wondrous city' – and had driven a bullock-cart for a merchant. He had also helped out a firework-maker, accompanying him to a great feast where he was giving a display. Unfortunately, amidst the many resplendent guests and ceremonial elephants decked out in gold and silver, the fireworks had all blown up together, killing eleven men, their manufacturer included. Kim had been hurled some distance, but was unharmed. He had then returned to Umballa – 'and so here' – as groom to a Sikh horseman.

Kim now asked nervously about Colonel Creighton, and whether he was still angry with him. Mahbub Ali smiled reassuringly. 'The Hand of Friendship has averted the Whip of Calamity,' he told Kim. But in future, he warned, 'when thou takest the Road it will be with me'. He then asked Kim how he intended to spend the rest of his holidays. 'I will come with thee, Mahbub Ali,' Kim replied contritely. Now a low-caste Hindu urchin travelling with a red-bearded Muslim horse-trader could hardly have failed to attract unwanted attention. Mahbub Ali therefore hurried Kim off to a shop he knew on the outskirts of Umballa where he transformed him, 'externally at least', into a Muslim urchin.

Next Mahbub Ali hired a room by the railway station, close to where his men and horses were camped, and there, over a meal from the bazaar and a water-pipe, he spoke to Kim, for the first time, about the Great Game. This was a subject which, until then, only Colonel Creighton himself had spoken of to Kim, on that long train journey down to Lucknow, and then somewhat obliquely, leaving him with little understanding of its real purpose. Kim now learned how the secret message he had delivered for Mahbub Ali to Creighton at his bungalow had enabled the authorities to nip in the bud the conspiracy of the five northern kings, and so avert a full-scale frontier war. It was, the Afghan added with pride, 'thanks to me – and thee'.

He discussed, too, with Kim the dangers facing those who played the Great Game. 'Our lives', he told him, 'lie in each other's hand.' That this was no exaggeration very quickly became apparent. For that night, while sleeping by the fire among Mahbub Ali's men, Kim overheard two mysterious strangers plotting in the darkness nearby to shoot the Afghan horse-trader: 'He must not go back beyond the passes a second time. It is the order.' Precisely how Kim, in the nick of time, succeeded in warning his friend, and how Mahbub Ali craftily turned the tables on the two assassins, is best read in the pages of *Kim*.

The next morning, taking the old tonga road, Mahbub

Ali and his small party set out for Simla, where they were to deliver horses. Kipling's rapturous description of that journey, as seen through the eyes of Kim, is profoundly evocative. For he knew and dearly loved that road, still recalling it vividly years after he had left India for good. Indeed, I defy anyone with an ounce of romance in their soul not to want to share it with Kim and Mahbub Ali. 'Kim', Kipling tells us, 'will remember it till he dies.' To him, born and brought up on India's sweltering plains, that slow climb up into the Himalayan foothills was a revelation, with 'its distant snows . . . the voices of a thousand water channels; the chatter of the monkeys; the solemn deodars; the vista of the plains rolled out far beneath them . . . all these things lifted Kim's heart to song within him'.

Today, sadly, the old tonga road up to Simla has crumbled away and, save in a few places, all but vanished. For it has long since been replaced by a modern tarmac road, and a narrow-gauge railway which climbs through no fewer than 103 individual tunnels. It is no longer possible, therefore, to try to follow in Kim's footsteps by pony, as I had hoped. By comparison, the meandering, six-hour rail journey from Kalka, just north of Umballa, to Simla is somewhat disappointing, sealed off as one is from the real world outside. Indeed, I must confess that it was with some relief that we emerged in our toy train from the penultimate tunnel and saw Simla, one-time summer capital of British India, at last swing into view. A few minutes later, though, my stupor was rudely shattered as a mob of frenzied porters, some climbing in through the open windows, invaded the train even before it had halted. Brushing aside protesting passengers, they seized their luggage, dragging it down on to the platform, or passing it out through the windows. From there, pursued by their breathless owners, the suitcases were swept away up the hill to hotels chosen by the porters, who thus collected not only a reluctant tip from the hapless passengers but also a commission from the hotel-owners. I only saved my own baggage from a like fate by quickly slamming shut the window – on the unfortunate porter's fingers, as it happened.

Whether, like Kim's, one's first glimpse of Simla comes from a bend on the old tonga road, or, like my own, from an approaching train, the view of the hill-station from a distance can have changed very little down the years. Surrounded by deodar forests, and strewn somewhat theatrically along a five-mile ridge, the town is a prisoner of its own geography, allowing its planners little or no room for manoeuvre or expansion. Its most prominent landmark today, as it has been for the past century and a half, is the handsome Anglican church, whose Victorian Gothic tower, a striking yellow in colour, can be seen from many miles away. With its Victorian-style town hall, mock-Tudor mansions and Gaiety Theatre, where once everything from Shakespeare to Noël Coward's latest hit could be seen, Simla is like bits of Godalming or Cheam airlifted 7,000 feet up into the Himalayas. But there is more to Simla than its mouldering British architecture. Just below the Mall, where the most fashionable, European-owned shops were once to be found, tier upon tier of little Indian shops cling like barnacles to the precipitous hillside, just as they did in Kim's day.

It was into this teeming labyrinth, known as the Lower Bazaar, that Kim and Mahbub Ali plunged. 'A man who knows his way there', wrote Kipling, 'can defy all the police of India's summer capital, so cunningly does veranda communicate with veranda, alleyway with alleyway, and bolt-hole

with bolt-hole.' In this human rabbit warren 'that climbs up from the valley to the Town Hall at an angle of forty-five', Kipling adds, 'are discussed by courtesans the things which are supposed to be profoundest secrets of the India Council'. This, in its turn, attracted 'the sub-sub-agents of half the Native States'. It was here that Mahbub Ali now hired himself a room, before breaking the news to Kim of what Colonel Creighton planned for him in Simla.

Until it was time for him to return to St Xavier's, Kim was to lodge in the house of one Lurgan Sahib. This, Mahbub Ali informed him, was a singular honour, for Lurgan Sahib himself had requested it. 'Men say', the Afghan added, 'he does magic.' Aware that Kim did not take kindly to discipline, Mahbub Ali impressed upon him that his little escapades were now over, and that Lurgan Sahib was one 'to be obeyed to the last wink of his eyelashes'. After purchasing him an ill-fitting set of European clothes, he told Kim how to find the Mall. There he was to ask where Lurgan Sahib lived. His final words of warning were that he must forget for a while 'that thou hast ever seen or spoken to me, Mahbub Ali, who sells horses to Colonel Creighton, whom thou dost not know'. Then, as Kim turned to leave, the Afghan muttered softly to himself: 'Here begins the Great Game.'

# 9

# The Secret World
of Simla

IN KIM'S DAY, despite its modest size and toy-town
appearance, Simla was one of the most powerful places
on the face of the earth. For seven months out of every twelve,
this cool Himalayan eyrie replaced sweltering Calcutta, and
later Delhi, as the capital of the mighty British Indian
Empire. From here, among the stately deodar trees and
breathtaking views of distant snows, a handful of white
moguls controlled the lives and destinies of a hundred million
Indians. And here too, at a time when fears of Cossack
regiments galloping down through the northern passes into
India were at their height, the largest, best-trained and most
formidable army in the whole of Asia had its headquarters.

Every year, as the heat on the plains below became unbearable, a mass migration of Europeans took place up to the
many hill-stations built along the southern slopes of the
Himalayas. But one particular exodus, which has been

likened to Hannibal's army crossing the Alps, was quite different from all the others. This was the annual departure for Simla of the Viceroy and his Council, together with their senior advisers, aides and families, not to mention cohorts of retainers. Towards the end of March or the beginning of April they made their way there from Calcutta, 1,200 miles away, by train, tonga, rickshaw and pony. Hot on their heels followed a small army of civil servants, Indian clerks and other functionaries, while behind them toiled a long baggage-train laden with filing cabinets and other official paraphernalia. 'Government out of a suitcase,' one Viceroy called it. Then, every October or November, the caravan rolled once more, bearing the Great Ones back to their splendid offices and residences in the winter capital, and their minions to more humble ones. And so it went on, year in and year out, from 1864 to 1939, when the practice ceased, though in 1911 the great trek was considerably shortened when Delhi replaced Calcutta as the new imperial capital.

But why, one may ask, was Simla chosen as India's summer capital in preference to any other hill-station, especially when it lay so far from Calcutta? In fact, several others had been seriously considered, including Darjeeling, which had the advantage of lying very much closer to Calcutta. However, this seeming advantage was outweighed by the fact that Simla was more centrally located, for Darjeeling, like Calcutta itself, was situated at the furthermost end of India. Since Calcutta was originally chosen as the capital, history had moved on, carrying India's centre of gravity westwards and northwards. Thus Simla, until then a small hill-village of little consequence, now lay closer than any of its rivals to India's most vulnerable frontier – that with Afghanistan. Furthermore, Simla's communications with the rest of India, whether by road, rail or telegraph, were excellent. Indeed, a network of some sixty routes led, directly or indirectly, to and from Simla, including one up to the Tibetan frontier. Finally there was the bracing climate, which was such – or so one Viceroy claimed – that he could do in a day in Simla what it would have taken him five days to do in the punishing summer heat of Calcutta.

In 1901, when *Kim* was first published, Kipling did not feel it necessary to so much as mention Simla's imperial role, or why it was that Colonel Creighton, Mahbub Ali and others still to come seemed to spend so much of their time there. Anyone literate enough to understand *Kim* would have been aware of the fact that, for more than half the year, it was the nerve-centre of the Raj, and that for the whole of the year it served as the headquarters of the Commander-in-Chief of the Indian Army. Only today, when Simla is simply another mouldering hill-station, shorn of all its imperial trappings and one-time grandeur and glamour, is it necessary to remind the reader of what it stood for when Kim made his way nervously up through the smoky bazaar towards the Mall, with its smart European-style shops and pretentious-looking town hall.

Kipling, it may be recalled, had a soft spot for Simla's Mall. For it was here, as a cub reporter of twenty-two, that he rode alone with the Commander-in-Chief, Lord Roberts of Kandahar, holder of the Victoria Cross for gallantry during the Indian Mutiny, who solicited his views on the state of morale in the army and other matters. It was to Simla, too, that Kipling owed much of his youthful fame as a writer of genius. For it was his merciless scrutiny of the Raj's private life there that gave birth to his celebrated collection of short stories, *Plain Tales from the Hills*. First published in 1888, when he was still only twenty-three, most of them had originally appeared in the *Civil and Military Gazette*, where they had enjoyed something of a *succès de scandale*. But it was their publication in book form, first in India and shortly afterwards in England, that attracted the attention of the literary world at home to the young writer's dazzling gifts.

The distinguished folklorist and anthropologist Andrew Lang declared that *Plain Tales from the Hills* threw more light on India – 'our task there' and 'the various people whom we try to rule' – than many of the government's official Blue Books. Others, however, especially those living on the spot, were considerably less enthusiastic, some getting very hot under the collar at this nosy young puppy's presumption in rummaging beneath the surface of Simla society. Sir Francis Younghusband, recalling his own youthful days in Simla, remembered Kipling being looked upon 'with great disfavour' by staff officers 'as being bumptious and above his station' – suggesting to a more modern reporter that he was probably doing a good job.

But *Kim*, written years later, explores a very different side of Simla. It is, as Sir Angus Wilson put it, 'one of the strangest novels ever written'. And much of its strangeness, as we shall see, derives from one extraordinary character –

Lurgan Sahib – to whom Kim is being sent for initiation into some of the more outlandish secrets of the Great Game. On entering Lurgan Sahib's house, led by a small Hindu boy he had encountered in the Mall, Kim brushed aside a heavy bead curtain to find himself face to face with a black-bearded man. Wearing a green eyeshade, he was sitting at a table in a pool of light threading pearls on to a silken string. For the mysterious Lurgan, among many other things rather less well known, dealt in precious stones and oriental antiques from his home, which also served as a shop, just off the Mall. One of the strange gifts that he possessed was the jealously guarded secret of restoring life and lustre to 'dead' or discoloured pearls. Because of this he was known as 'the healer of sick pearls'.

Looking up at Kim, he removed his eyeshade and stared intently at him for a full half-minute without uttering a word. Kim noticed that the pupils of his eyes dilated widely and then shrank to mere pinpricks. This was clearly intended to unsettle him, for Lurgan then told him not to be afraid. But Kim had seen this trick performed before – by a Lahore fakir who did it for money. 'Why should I fear?' he answered boldly. He had passed his first test – the first of many, each stranger than the one before, to which Lurgan Sahib was to subject him in the days ahead.

The pages which follow are among the most unforgettable and fascinating in the whole of *Kim*, a wonderful mixture of the exotic and the mysterious – heady, seductive stuff to a teenager in love with the East, as I was when I first read *Kim*. Angus Wilson likens the goings-on in Lurgan's shop to Fagin's kitchen and his instruction of Oliver in the art of thieving. But although a clever comparison, it excludes some of the most beguiling and fantastic elements that Kipling, himself fascinated by Eastern mysticism and the supernatural, wove into his tale. Lurgan's shop, he tells us, was filled with things 'that smelt like all the temples of the East', and Kim's nostrils detected 'a whiff of musk, a puff of sandalwood, and a breath of sickly jessamine oil'.

Beyond the circle of light on his table, however, Lurgan's shop was in darkness. He now raised the lamp so that Kim could see the rest of the room and its grotesque contents. 'As the light swept them,' wrote Kipling, 'there leaped out from the walls a collection of Tibetan devil-dance masks . . . horned masks, scowling masks, and masks of idiotic terror.' Kim, Lurgan informed him, would be sleeping on the floor beneath these nightmarish apparitions. Clearly this was intended to test his nerve. But Kim was not that easily intimidated by such things, designed though they were to induce fear in people. For he, like Kipling, was already familiar with them from the 'Wonder House' at Lahore.

Not all the treasures in Lurgan's shop, though, were as loathsome as those masks, with their 'fiend-embroidered draperies'. There were prayer-wheels and ghost-daggers also from Tibet, Russian samovars 'with turquoises on the lid', gilt figures of Buddha, little portable lacquer altars, yellow ivory crucifixes 'from Japan of all places', Persian water-jugs 'for the hands after meals', bales of oriental rugs 'smelling atrociously', weapons of every variety, incense-burners 'with friezes of fantastic devils running round them', incense-sticks in jars 'crusted over with raw garnets', and 'a thousand other oddments' either in show-cases or simply piled up or thrown into a corner.

One can imagine the joy with which Kipling compiled this inventory of artefacts from his recollections of the Lahore museum, where – or so he claimed – he once served as unpaid deputy curator for six weeks when his father was away. It is hard to imagine, though, how he managed this at the same time as working for ten to fifteen hours a day on the *Civil and Military Gazette*, of which he represented 'fifty per cent of the editorial staff' – the editor representing the other fifty per cent. But perhaps it was written tongue-in-cheek, and he was merely custodian of the keys to the old 'Wonder House', then a comparatively modern institution. Nonetheless, as we know from his loving description of the Graeco-Buddhist sculptures in the opening chapter of *Kim*, he was extremely familiar with its contents, and almost certainly 'borrowed' from these, perhaps with his father's help, when describing Lurgan Sahib's shop.

Although, so far, Kim had passed Lurgan's tests of elementary courage, there was far worse to follow; with ghostly voices crying out in the night, close to where Kim slept. But to describe these, and how Kim dealt with their perpetrator, would be to spoil the story. Likewise, some of Lurgan's other tests designed to gauge Kim's fitness for the Great Game, including trial by hypnosis, would lose in the telling if I were to attempt it. One test, however, is too well known to be spoiled by describing it, and that is the one which has become known – to generations of Boy Scouts and Girl Guides – as 'Kim's Game'. Kipling, and Lurgan Sahib, call it the 'Jewel Game', and it so impressed Lord Baden-Powell that he adopted it, in 1908, as part of Boy Scout training.

It is here that the small Hindu boy who had led Kim to Lurgan's house re-enters the narrative. He had, it appears, been sent to the Mall to spot the new arrival and bring him back, for he too lived in the house. His role is somewhat ambiguous, but he seems to have been half servant and half guinea-pig for Lurgan's mysterious experiments, a kind of sorcerer's apprentice. Angus Wilson, who was himself a homosexual, detected 'obvious sexual undertones' in Lurgan's relationship with the Hindu boy. But then he also sees such undertones in Mahbub Ali's fondness for Kim, whom he notes is 'remarkably physically beautiful' – though in fact this only emerges much later in the book, after Kim has left

St Xavier's. Such matters, however, are beyond the scope of my own narrative.

Playing the 'Jewel Game', which Lurgan had devised to test and train the memories of Great Game initiates, involved placing an assortment of gems and other objects on a tray, and then seeing how many could be remembered after one minute's observation. Fifteen small treasures selected by Lurgan were thus placed before Kim and the Hindu boy and then covered up. Kim, feeling well pleased with himself, was able to recall and describe all but one of these. To his fury, however, the Hindu boy was able to remember them all and to describe each one in considerably greater detail. Kim protested that the test was unfair as the Hindu boy was far more familiar with jewels than he. 'If it were men – or horses,' he insisted, then he would easily have won. So they played it again, using everyday objects, but again the Hindu boy won. Order, not to mention Kim's pride, was only restored when Lurgan explained the secret of the Hindu boy's success. The game had to be played 'many times over till it is done perfectly – for it is worth doing'. After that the two boys practised it every morning, 'sometimes with piles of swords and daggers, sometimes with photographs of natives'.

In the afternoons they played a slightly different game of Lurgan's devising. From behind a screen they silently observed the steady stream of customers and other visitors to his shop, and at the end of the day he would make them give a detailed description of each one, together with an assessment of his character 'as shown in his face, talk and manner', together with their notion of 'his real errand'. In the evenings they played a third game – disguise. After Lurgan had made up their faces – 'with a brush dab here and a line there changing them past recognition' – they would dress up in the many garments and turbans which he kept in the shop, and pose as individuals of greatly differing backgrounds. Lurgan would explain in minute detail exactly 'how such and such a caste talked, or walked, or coughed, or spat, or sneezed'. Here Kim far outshone the Hindu boy, even teaching Lurgan a few things which he had picked up in the Lahore bazaars. Once, disguised as a fakir of a particular caste, he sat immobile for half an hour – 'cross-legged, ash-smeared, and wild-eyed'. So delighted was Lurgan by his performance that he brought in to observe it a Bengali friend, an extraordinary figure named Hurree Chunder Mookerjee, also known as the Babu, or R17, of whom we shall see a good deal more, and at whom Kim directed a colourful stream of beggar's chat.

It was now time for Kim to return to St Xavier's. But before bidding him farewell, Lurgan spoke frankly to him about the Great Game and those who played it. 'From time to time,' he said, 'God causes men to be born – and thou art one of them – who have a lust to go abroad at the risk of their lives and discover news – today it may be of far-off things, tomorrow of some hidden mountain, and the next day of some nearby men who have done a foolishness against the state. These souls are very few; and of these few, not more than ten are of the best.' Of these ten, he added, one was Hurree Chunder Mookerjee. 'He is a writer of tales for a certain colonel . . . and it is noticeable that he has no name, but only a number and a letter – that is a custom among us.' The Babu, he informed Kim, would be sharing a tonga with him down to the plains, from where he would catch the train to Lucknow.

This seems an appropriate moment for us to pause for a while and investigate the origins, in Kipling's mind, of that remarkable creation Lurgan Sahib. So strange is he that one might be forgiven for assuming that he is a total invention. But one would be wrong. For like all the other leading players in Kipling's Great Game cast, he too was modelled on a living individual – one, moreover, even more extraordinary than any of the others. Like Lurgan, he was a dealer in rare gems living in Simla, where he conducted his business from his home. And like Lurgan – according to his obituary in *The Times* of January 17, 1921 – he was 'a most valuable helper of the political secret service', though in precisely what fashion its anonymous author does not reveal. Of one thing, however, one can be fairly certain. For *The Times* to accept, or commission, such an obituary, especially in those days, it would have had to have had absolute confidence in the contributor's command of the facts. It is this that makes the rest of his revelations so interesting, for it must be one of the strangest obituaries ever to appear in that, or any other, newspaper.

A. M. Jacob (no one appears to have known what his initials stood for) rose, we are told, 'from slavery to fame and immense wealth', but died in obscurity and poverty at the age of seventy-one. He was, we are assured categorically, the model for Kipling's Lurgan Sahib. 'Mystery', the writer goes on, 'surrounds his origin as well as many features of his career.' Claiming to be a Turk, he was believed by some to be of Armenian or Polish Jewish parentage, though born in Turkey. 'He was of the humblest origin,' the obituarist continues, 'and when ten years old was sold as a slave to a rich pasha who, discovering the boy's uncommon abilities, made a student of him.' He thus acquired the foundation of his intimate knowledge of Eastern life, languages, art, literature and occultism. 'On gaining manumission on the death of his master . . . he made the pilgrimage to Mecca in disguise, and worked a passage from Jeddah to Bombay.' There he landed 'with hardly enough money in his pocket for his next meal', but luckily obtained a clerkship to 'a great nobleman' at the Nizam of Hyderabad's court. A profitable deal over a precious stone enabled him to move to Delhi and set up as a gem-dealer, a trade from which he quickly amassed a small fortune. In the 1870s, seeing greater scope there for his business, he moved to Simla, where he soon became a legendary figure, thanks to his singular gifts and supposed occult powers.

'He was endowed with a wonderfully handsome face and form,' *The Times* obituary continues, while 'there was about him a compelling magnetism and power and mystery, which led to him being sought for conversation and advice by viceroys and princes.' His unrivalled knowledge of precious stones, moreover, gave him a clientele that included 'the highest in the land', while his Simla home, which was 'furnished in the most lavish Oriental style and filled with priceless ornaments', was thronged with distinguished visitors. 'Yet his own habits', we are told, 'were ascetic almost to the verge of sternness.' A vegetarian, a teetotaller and a non-smoker, Jacob lived, according to one viceroy, 'like a skeleton in a jewel room'. Despite owning a stable of excellent mounts (and this comes from another source), he preferred to ride a favourite shaggy hill pony. He could (and this, too, comes from another source) speak English, French, Turkish, Persian, Arabic and Urdu with 'considerable fluency'. But all this is quite commonplace compared to some of his other attributes. These are no more than hinted at in *The Times*, which refers to the 'miracles' with which he astonished his guests, adding that 'even the late Mme Blavatsky had to admit his superiority in providing at will supernatural phenomena'.

For the bizarre details of Jacob's 'miracles' one must turn to the pages of the *Pioneer*, which then maintained a correspondent at Simla, and whose editor was deeply interested in the occult, as was Kipling himself. Jacob, it reported, could make himself invisible at will, leaving his dinner guests watching the movements of his knife and fork, which remained visible. On another occasion, the *Pioneer* recorded, he was asked by a general attending one of his dinner parties to show them some tricks. Annoyed by his use of the word 'tricks', Jacob ordered his servant to fetch the general's thick, grapevine stick and a glass bowl filled with water, which he placed on the table before his guests. He then thrust the stick, handle downwards, into the bowl. 'After a time,' the newspaper tells us, 'they saw numbers of shoots, like rootlets, begin issuing from the handle until they filled the bowl and held the stick steady, Jacob standing over it, muttering all the time.' Then a crackling sound was heard, and young twigs started to sprout from the upper part of the general's stick. Soon these were covered with leaves and flowers. Next the flowers turned into small bunches of black grapes, which fattened and ripened before their eyes. When the 'miracle' was complete – it took some ten minutes in all – a servant bore the vine around the guests, who helped themselves to its fruit, one or two slipping grapes into their pockets to taste at home, lest they were the victims of hypnosis or mesmerism of some kind.

But that, according to the *Pioneer*, was not all. Jacob now ordered one of his guests to close his eyes and imagine himself back in his bedroom at his own bungalow, which lay a mile away. The man did so. 'Now open your eyes,' he was told. To his utter astonishment he found that he was indeed in his own home, and that Jacob was standing beside him. Jacob next ordered him to close his eyes again, so that they could rejoin the other guests. Convinced that he had been hypnotised, and wishing to see how Jacob would get himself out of the difficulty, he refused. 'Oh well,' Jacob replied, 'since you won't come, I must go alone. Goodbye.' With that he vanished. What was happening to the other guests during their absence we are not told. Nor are we given the names or identities of any of them, except that the general was 'well-known'.

Nowadays, of course, no one would believe such tales, nor would any respectable newspaper print them. But this, it should be remembered, was at a time when there was intense public interest in occult phenomena, greatly stimulated by the psychic claims and demonstrations of Madame Helena Blavatsky, a Russian occultist, who had lived for a while in Simla, where she conducted seances and produced the manifestations that made her world-famous. Kipling's father, it might be added, told his son that he considered her 'one of the most interesting and unscrupulous impostors' he had ever met, and subsequently her 'tricks' were exposed. This did nothing, however, to diminish Kipling's relish for the occult, which was to intensify following the death of two of his three children at an early age. His creation of the mysterious Lurgan Sahib out of the even more mysterious Jacob Sahib – whom he may well have known in his Simla days – is just one of many examples to be found in his writings of this lifelong fascination with the supernatural.

Whatever the truth about Jacob's own supernatural powers, these proved incapable of saving him from financial ruin following a sensational court case that he brought in 1891 against the Nizam of Hyderabad, then reputed to be the richest man on earth. At the centre of the dispute was one of the world's biggest diamonds – the Victoria, also known as the Imperial – which Jacob had sold and personally delivered to the Nizam at his palace. Jacob claimed, successfully, that he had been paid only half the agreed price of £300,000. However, although he won the case, he was unable to obtain restitution, for the British courts had no jurisdiction over the Indian princes. This, together with his massive legal costs run up during the fifty-seven-day hearing, eventually drove him into bankruptcy. His downfall was accelerated by the defaulting of other Indian princes, or the withdrawal of their patronage. The unfortunate Jacob was finally forced to sell all the treasures and jewels he had amassed over many years, often for a fraction of their true value, and move to Bombay where, now a broken man, he eked out a meagre living dealing in old china. For some years he suffered from blindness, which was finally cured by the charity of a surgeon friend. India Office records show that he died on January 9, 1921, and is buried somewhere in Bombay's vast Sewri cemetery. No photograph of him, so far as I can discover, exists.

Jacob thus remained an enigma to the very end, though he is known to have kept detailed diaries for much of his life, filled with the secrets of his strange career. One day, perhaps, these will come to light, possibly on the dusty shelves of some second-hand bookshop in Bombay, or on a stall in the bazaar. After all, stranger things have happened in that bazaar. In the 1950s, six topographical watercolours of India's northern borders painted by the murdered Great Game player George Hayward were found in the Bombay bazaar, eighty years after his death and 1,200 miles from the spot where he was killed. How these paintings, which were subsequently sold at auction in London, found their way there remains a mystery.

Curiously enough, as I write this, the Jacob saga has taken a sudden new twist. Again it arises from a bitter legal dispute involving the Nizam of Hyderabad, great-grandson of the one to whom Jacob sold the Victoria diamond, and that same glittering stone. Declaring it a national treasure in 1972, together with a hoard of 172 other pieces from the Nizam's collection, the Indian government compulsorily purchased the lot, thereby preventing it from being sold on the international market. They first offered £15 million for it, but were eventually forced to raise this to £40 million on the orders of the Indian Supreme Court after twenty years of legal wrangling. However, both Sotheby's and Christie's have valued the collection, were it to be publicly auctioned, at around £250 million. The present Nizam and his family understandably feel that they have been cheated of their birthright, and put this down to the fact that they are Muslims and that they no longer wield the immense power that they did in British times.

By far the most valuable item in the entire hoard, say Sotheby's, is the Victoria diamond, weighing in at a massive 184.5 metric carats, and for the possession of which the Nizam had only parted with £150,000. Today it is valued by Sotheby's at £100 million. For years the present Nizam's grandfather used it as a paperweight, having discovered it hidden in the toe of his own father's slipper after the latter's death. It may be of some comfort to Jacob – wherever he is, and if his psychic powers continue to function from beyond the grave – to know that the descendants of the man who cheated him more than a century ago have themselves been diddled. Nor is that all. Jacob may never have got his money, and the case may have cost him his career and fortune, but he has been assured of immortality, at least in the dazzling world of diamonds. The massive gem that he sold to the Nizam, and which was flown to Delhi on a special aircraft after its purchase by the Indian government, is no longer known as the Victoria or the Imperial diamond, but has been renamed the Jacob diamond.

Kipling was not alone in perceiving in the exotic figure of Jacob the raw material for a fictional character. For Jacob is clearly recognisable in at least two other Victorian novels set in Simla. He appears in F. Marion Crawford's *Mr Isaacs*, published in 1882, as the mysterious Persian dealer in precious stones after whom the book is named. Sixteen years later he resurfaced in Colonel Newnham Davis's *Jadoo* – meaning magic – this time as an occultist-ascetic 'who knows more of the mystic secrets of India than any other man', and who 'hears things that other men cannot hear, and sees things other men cannot see'. Both novels, like *Kim*, were published when Jacob was still living in Simla, though how he reacted to such exposure is not known.

All three novelists naturally took different facets of Jacob's remarkable career and personality from which to construct their own character. Kipling, it appears, had got wind of the fact that he had worked for the Indian government in an undercover capacity, and so recruits him in *Kim* as Colonel Creighton's right-hand man. Evidence of Jacob having been involved in the Great Game, or some kind of intelligence work, is to be found in Edward Buck's much respected *Simla Past and Present*, first written, on Lord Curzon's suggestion, in 1904. As a long-term resident of Simla himself, and also as Reuter correspondent there, Buck appears to have known Jacob quite well. Four years after the latter's death, in an updated edition of his book, Buck disclosed: 'From papers which Mr Jacob showed me there is no doubt in my mind that he was at one time treated as a secret agent of Government in certain matters.' Precisely what these 'matters' were, Buck, who was later knighted for his services to the Raj, is too discreet to say. He hints, however, that the answer to this and to the numerous other riddles surrounding Jacob lies buried somewhere in the records of what he calls 'the mysterious Secret Department' of the Indian government. Needless to say, at that time, these ultra-secret files were totally inaccessible, though today, with a few exceptions, they are freely available to scholars.

One day, when I have more time, I might embark on the mammoth task of working my way through thirty years of these archives – today in the India Office Records, part of the British Library – in the hope of uncovering the truth about Jacob. Until then, or until someone else attempts it, he will remain an enigma. But there is one small mystery which has still to be addressed. Where exactly was the shop in which Kim underwent his initiation into the secrets of the Great Game at the hands of Lurgan Sahib? It was my attempt to solve this, more than anything else, which brought me to this ghost-town of the Raj.

# 10

# Lurgan Sahib's Vanishing Shop

DESPITE HIS VIVID and detailed description of Lurgan Sahib's shop interior, and the bizarre things which went on there, Kipling offers us few real clues as to its whereabouts in this straggling hill-station. It lay, as we know from *Kim*, a short walk from the town hall, though just how short and in which direction we can only guess. We know that one entered it via a veranda which was 'flush with the main road'. But which main road? We also know that the rear of it was 'built out over the sheer hillside', and that its occupants 'looked down into their neighbours' chimney-pots'. That, however, applies to almost every house or shop in Simla. Lastly, we know from Mahbub Ali, when he was briefing Kim on how to find it, that it lay among the European shops, and that 'all Simla knows it'.

But if 'all Simla' knew where it was in Mahbub Ali's day, they certainly do not now, though some guidebooks suggest that you need merely ask to have it pointed out to you. 'Just near Clarkes Hotel, on the corner,' one esteemed guidebook confidently informs the visitor to Simla. Yet when I asked the hotel's general manager, Mr Raman Khanna, to point it out to me he smiled and shook his head. British guests, he told me, often asked the whereabouts of Lurgan Sahib's shop, but he was unable to tell them.

What we are really looking for, of course, is Jacob's old shop, on which Kipling appears to have modelled, with modifications, Lurgan's extraordinary establishment, just as he created Lurgan out of Jacob. To find Jacob's shop – 'a quaint little shop on the Mall', Buck calls it – shouldn't, I reasoned, prove too difficult. To be on the safe side, though, I had allocated two whole days to the task. I began by approaching a number of respected individuals who had lived all their lives in Simla, and who were familiar with *Kim*. But while they were agreed that Jacob had lived in a largish house on the edge of town called Belvedere (which happened to be next door to where I was staying), there was considerable disagreement as to where his shop had stood. The result was that, with my time running out fast, I was sent off on all sorts of false trails and in unlikely directions. It soon became clear to me that, despite their insistence, none of them had the slightest idea where this shop, so famous in its day, was to be found.

I then approached a number of the longer-established shops on the Mall. These included a jeweller, a bookseller and a photographer who sold old sepia prints of Simla, and who I hoped might, by some miracle, have one showing

Jacob's shopfront. But the result was equally disappointing. I had now used up one of my two precious days and seemed as far away from my goal as ever. I next turned to the public library to see whether they had any old guidebooks, ideally

locally produced ones, which I might have missed in London before setting out. I hoped at least to come upon an old advertisement for Jacob's business, or a photograph of a row of shops, one of which might bear his name. But once again I drew a blank, although my hopes were briefly raised when I came across a list of businesses, dating back to Jacob's days in Simla, with premises on the Mall. There were two jewellers listed – Hamilton & Co., and Charles Nephew Co. – but no Jacob.

By this time I had begun to wonder whether, like Lurgan Sahib, Jacob operated from home, that is from Belvedere, where he threw his smart dinner parties and performed his 'miracles'. Indeed, had it not been for Buck's categorical assertion that he dwelt at Belvedere but also had a shop on the Mall, I might have settled gratefully for this solution. As it happened, though, Buck was not alone in insisting that Jacob owned a shop in town. In 1913, an American who had lived for several years in Simla produced, under the pen-name Doz, a somewhat eccentric and whimsical guide to the town called *Simla in Ragtime*. In this he confirms the existence of Jacob's shop, though his description of its precise where-abouts is so confusing as to be almost incomprehensible. Again, in 1957, another American – a member of the august Kipling Society – sought to clear the matter up by drawing a map on which he pinpointed Lurgan Sahib's shop, together with various other 'Kipling sites' in Simla. Unfortunately he provides no supporting evidence for his choice of location, and admits that it is little more than conjecture. He makes no reference, moreover, to ever having been to Simla.

On my way back from the library, pondering my next move, I came upon a comical sight in the Mall. Simla, as everyone who has been there knows, has all but been taken over by troupes of large and mischievous monkeys who thun-der across the corrugated-iron rooftops and poke their hairy faces into almost everything. Indeed, so familiar are the people of Simla with these aliens – an overflow from the monkey temple up the hill – that they hardly seem to notice them. To visitors, however, their antics are at times hilarious. Sitting sketching on a wall that afternoon was a modern English memsahib in a floppy white sun-hat. Seated beside her, earnestly admiring her work, were two very large monkeys. After a minute or two they grew bored and scampered off, much to the artist's relief.

As it happened, this was the second simian burlesque I had been treated to that day. My bathroom window overlooked the playground of a boy's prep-school, where I observed hosts of young Kims, in smart blazers and shorts, clambering excitedly on swings and climbing frames while awaiting the bell for assembly. As they disappeared inside, a troupe of monkeys who had been watching impatiently from the trees descended on the playground and began to cavort on the swings and frames just like the boys, only they were better at it. The same performance presumably took place every morning, though after a few minutes the monkeys tired of it and took off to look for fresh mischief. One only hopes they were not off on a baby-snatching expedition. For I read only recently in an obituary notice how a distinguished Raj official nearly had his career cut short at an early age when a monkey tried to grab him from his cradle through an open window. Indeed, so troublesome were these creatures to the British – who viewed them as anything but sacred – that until Independence the Simla police maintained a secret 'monkey incident' file. Such secrecy, necessary to avoid inflaming local Hindu susceptibilities, raises suspicions of covert culling operations at dead of night.

After following so many false trails in search of Jacob's shop, I was now forced to concede that I had failed in my mission to Simla, and must press on in pursuit of Kim. I was fairly confident that on my return to London a day or two among the archives of the India Office Library would give me the answer. After all, there was no one still living in Simla who could possibly have remembered Jacob's shop, and any claims could only be hearsay, requiring thorough checking against the records of the time. I retreated to my hotel to lick my wounds before packing for my journey back down to the plains in Kim's footsteps. On the way I halted for the last time outside Belvedere, the extraordinary Jacob's one-time home, and tried hard to imagine what it must have been like in his day, with his liveried servants, VIP guests and occult dinner parties. But the passage of time – it all took place a century or more ago – has effectively obliterated any traces of Belvedere's mysterious past. Today it is a fashionable high school for girls, with a smart new frontage and little, if any, of its original character. If ever a house called for a ghost – and a number in Simla are reputed to be haunted – it is surely Belvedere. But however strongly poor Jacob might be drawn to the scene of his former glories, it is unlikely that this highly secretive and fastidious man would be able to face the teenage clamour which today bursts forth from his old home.

Unlike Kim, I took a taxi from Simla down to the plains. I had no wish to repeat my seemingly interminable six-hour rail marathon, with its 103 tunnels and wearisome halts, of a few days earlier. Kim himself took the old road, now long vanished, sharing a tonga with Lurgan Sahib's obese and jolly Bengali friend, Hurree Chunder Mookerjee, known as the Babu for short. He was mystified, however, as to how this overweight and talkative Hindu could possibly be, as Lurgan had insisted, one of the ten best players in the Great Game. But he, like us, knew very little then about this shrewd and deceptive individual who, when engaged in shadowy tasks for 'a certain colonel', bore the number R17 instead of a name. One day, Kim reflected, he too would have a letter and a number, or so Lurgan Sahib had promised. He might even – like Mahbub Ali – have a price on his head.

At Kalka, before going their own ways, they shared a copious meal, during which the Babu, having reminded Kim that he himself was an MA of Calcutta University, held forth at length on the virtues of a good education and of being widely read in the English classics. He went on to tell Kim a little more of what awaited him on leaving St Xavier's and joining the élite few who worked for Colonel Creighton. At times, he explained, it might be 'inexpedient' for him to be caught carrying map-making equipment. However, by knowing the exact length of his own pace, he would be able, secretly and accurately, to measure great distances simply by walking, storing this information by slipping a bead on his Buddhist rosary at every thousandth pace.

Finally, after talking non-stop for an hour and a half, the genial Bengali presented Kim with a small farewell gift. It was a heart-shaped brass box normally used for carrying betel-nut and other Indian spices. However, this one contained instead tiny bottles filled with medicines and drugs, including quinine, which might one day save his own life were he to fall ill, or be used to cure others when posing as a native doctor or holy man. After explaining their use, the Babu slipped away as 'noiselessly as a cat', despite his enormous bulk, while Kim set off on his long train journey back to St Xavier's.

*

The reader may have begun to wonder what has become of the lama in all this time. Indeed, he has now been absent from *Kim* for more than forty pages, causing the first-time reader to suspect that perhaps he has already fulfilled his role in the narrative. Happily, this is not so. The reason for his absence is simply that he is waiting, with meritorious patience, for his *chela* to complete his education as a sahib, for only then will they be able to resume their search together for the River of the Arrow. Without his *chela*, he has learned through a dream, he has little chance of ever finding it. Instead, therefore, using the Tirthankars' temple at Benares as his base, he has embarked on a series of journeys across India in the sacred footsteps of the Buddha. In the course of one of these he even returns for a day to Lahore to see his white-bearded friend, the Keeper of Images at the 'Wonder House'. The latter, Kipling tells us (of the man, it will be recalled, whom he modelled on his own father), 'has still in his possession a most marvellous account of his wanderings and meditations'. As the lama, too, is modelled on an actual Tibetan lama who visited the museum, according to Lockwood Kipling's letter to Sir Aurel Stein, one finds oneself wondering whether such an account did, in fact, once exist. If so, it does not appear to be among Lockwood's papers, though it could possibly lie – in the form of notes taken down by him – long-forgotten in the archives of the Lahore museum, or have been among those many items grudgingly surrendered to India, as the birthplace of Buddha and Buddhism, in 1947.

On returning from these pilgrimages, 'a little thinner and a shade yellower, if that were possible', the lama would take the train to Lucknow to visit his *chela* at St Xavier's, as he had promised on that painful day of separation outside the Gates of Learning. Once, they spent an entire day down by the banks of the Gumti river, with Kim vainly and tearfully pleading with the Tibetan to be allowed to accompany him for a month – even 'for a little week' – during the next school holidays. Kim's St Xavier record, Kipling tells us, reveals that on this occasion he was punished for playing truant for a day 'in the company of a street beggar'. Apart from a few other such minor transgressions, Kim's end-of-term reports – sent to Colonel Creighton and Father Victor – showed him to be an assiduous and conscientious pupil, with a considerable gift for mathematics and map-making. He also played football enthusiastically for the school First Eleven.

But if Colonel Creighton and Father Victor were pleased with Kim's progress at St Xavier's, Mahbub Ali was far less struck by the sahibs' system of education, being himself brought up in what Lord Curzon called 'the frontier school of character'. For such a rarity as Kim, whose uncanny potential for secret service work the Afghan had been the first to spot, a white man's schooling was, he felt, largely a waste of precious time. Indeed, more than once he had argued the case with Creighton, declaring: 'Colonel Sahib, only once in a thousand years is a horse born so well fitted for the game as this our colt. And we need men.' He would have preferred to have taken Kim, to whom he was greatly attached, under his own wing, and taught him all that he had learned of the Great Game. In the event a compromise was struck. It was agreed by all three parties – Creighton, Mahbub and Kim himself – that during all future school holidays he would be given what today would be called 'work experience', accompanying the Afghan on some of his less hazardous missions, and receiving further training from Lurgan Sahib in Simla.

Accordingly, during his next holidays, he and Mahbub Ali delivered a large batch of horses to Bombay, after which they went by coastal steamer to Karachi, from where they travelled on up to Quetta. Here Mahbub Ali put some of Kim's newly acquired Great Game skills to the test. Posing as an illiterate scullion boy, he spent the next four days in the home of a suspected arms smuggler. The latter, Mahbub knew, stored the secrets of his illegal dealings in a small vellum-bound volume. These Mahbub – or, to be more precise, Colonel Creighton – was extremely anxious to peruse. While the household slept, Kim painstakingly copied out the entire contents of the ledger – 'by moonlight, lying behind an outhouse, all through one hot night' – before slipping away and meeting Mahbub six miles down the road. To Kim the entries had seemed innocent enough, consisting simply of livestock sales. In fact, the delighted Mahbub explained to him, these were not camel and cattle sales, but consignments of rifles bound for the north, and part of a far wider traffic in such arms. 'The Game', he told Kim, 'is so large that one sees but little of it at a time.'

Most of the Christmas holidays Kim spent with Lurgan Sahib in Simla – by now under four feet of snow – perfecting the various disguises and impersonations, whether of Muslim priest or Hindu doctor, that he might be required to adopt. He was made to learn by heart and recite entire chapters of the Koran 'till he could deliver them with the very roll and cadence of a mullah'. Lurgan also taught him the names and properties of many native drugs, and the correct incantation to recite when administering them. In the evenings, Kipling tells us, 'he wrote charms on parchment – elaborate pentagrams crowned with the names of devils – Murra, and Awan the Companion of Kings – all fantastically written in the corners'. Finally, Lurgan explained to Kim how to look after his own health, showing him fever cures and other 'simple remedies of the Road'. Then, just when Kim believed it was all over, Colonel Creighton set him a surveying exam, testing his knowledge of 'rods and chains and links and angles'.

However, the following school holidays Kim again spent with Mahbub Ali, whom he accompanied on camelback to the mysterious walled city of Bikanir, then the capital of a remote feudal kingdom the size of England, which lay in the middle of the great Rajasthan desert. While the Afghan bought and sold horses there, Kim – on Colonel Creighton's orders – secretly mapped this ancient caravan city. This had, necessarily, to be a classic pundit-style operation. For Muslim horse-boys (Kim was posing as Mahbub Ali's nephew) 'are not', in Kipling's words, 'expected to drag survey-chains round the capital of an independent native state'. He was forced, therefore, to pace out all his measurements and record them, not in a notebook, but discreetly on his prayer-beads. Again, for the same reason, his compass bearings had to be taken after dusk. It was Kim's first attempt to make a map under such circumstances, and his efforts were not wholly successful, causing Mahbub Ali to laugh greatly before setting him his next task. This was to prepare a written report, in the back of the ledger that Mahbub kept under the flap of his camel saddle, on 'everything that thou hast seen or touched or considered'. It should be written, Mahbub told Kim, as though the Commander-in-Chief himself was coming 'with a vast army' to attack the city.

But Kim, even at the age of sixteen, was quick to spot the Afghan's trap. 'How great an army?' he asked Mahbub. Fifty thousand men, the latter replied. 'Folly!' declared Kim, remembering how they themselves had nearly perished on their own desert crossing, so few and so bad were the wells. 'Not a thousand thirsty men,' he told Mahbub triumphantly, could survive such a crossing, let alone fifty times that number. With that he sat down in a room with a good lock which Mahbub had hired by the main city gateway, and penned his report in 'its unmistakable St Xavier's running script'. Together with Kim's map, Kipling assures us, this is to be found in Colonel Creighton's secret service records (albeit wrongly filed 'by a careless clerk' under another agent's name, or rather number). But by now, Kipling warns those who might seek to find it, 'the pencil characters must be almost illegible'.

Kim and Mahbub Ali's return journey southwards, across the great salt desert to Jodhpur, was no less gruelling than their outward one had been. 'They marched', wrote Kipling, 'jaw-bound against blowing sand.' Today the journey to Bikanir, while exhausting, is pretty tame by comparison. For there is now a railway across the desert, with an overnight sleeper that leaves Delhi at 9 p.m. and reaches Bikanir eleven and a half hours later. Many visitors, however, include it in a tour of the other Rajasthan desert cities, travelling by air-conditioned coach, with a guest-lecturer steeped in the region's exotic history and architecture in tow. But few nowadays associate Bikanir with Kim and Mahbub Ali, or attempt to count their paces on a string of prayer-beads as they circumnavigate its massive red sandstone walls. Indeed, sensation-seekers are more likely to be drawn to Bikanir by its unique Rat Temple where dwell, and are worshipped, literally thousands of these sacred rodents, which live behind silver doors and are fed by their devotees on sweetmeats, milk and grain. The temple floor is richly carpeted with their droppings and, as shoes are forbidden, visitors are advised to take thick socks which can be disposed of afterwards. But rats, warns one guidebook, 'create a powerful odour, and few visitors will wish to linger for long'.

On their second night's halt, as Kim and Mahbub struggled home across the desert, the Afghan suddenly reached into his saddle-bag and drew out a brand-new set of clothing. It was such as might be worn by a stylish young blood of Mahbub's tribe. This was what Mahbub called 'a dress of honour', making Kim an honorary Pathan, and it was his reward for graduating in the art of clandestine surveying. And that was not all. Mahbub now produced from his saddle-bag a nickel-plated, pearl-handled revolver of .45 calibre. This, he told Kim as he handed it to him, 'takes government bullets', which could easily be found, 'especially across the border'. Warning Kim always to keep the revolver hidden beneath his clothing, Mahbub added: 'and please God, thou shalt some day kill a man with it'.

Kim was speechless – 'his heart too full for words' – for he had never owned such treasures as these. As he donned the Pathan costume, Mahbub clapped him on the shoulder and laughed: 'Oh, the hearts to be broken!' The gifts, Kim knew, were also Mahbub's acknowledgement that he had reached manhood, which comes early among the tribes of the North-West Frontier. But on remembering that he had shortly to return to St Xavier's, his euphoria faded. 'When I go back to the *madrissah*', he told Mahbub, as he lovingly fondled the shiny new revolver, 'I must return it.' The Afghan would have to look after it for him, for firearms, he explained, were strictly forbidden at St Xavier's. Here Kim had touched on one of his old friend's most sensitive spots. 'Son,' the Afghan declared with indignation, 'I am wearied of this *madrissah*, where they take the best years of a man to teach him what he can only learn on the Road.'

Soon it was time for Kim to take the train to Lucknow,

having first stepped out of his tribal clothes and into those of a St Xavier's boy. Mahbub Ali, after sadly watching Kim depart for a world he could never fully understand, turned angrily on his heel, determined to have the matter out, once and for all, with Colonel Creighton and Lurgan Sahib.

# II

# *Jacob Strikes Back*

L EAVING MAHBUB ALI heading up to Simla to confront
Colonel Creighton, and Kim in his second-class railway
compartment bound for St Xavier's, I meanwhile had
returned to London to try finally to solve the riddle of Lurgan
Sahib's mysterious shop. I was confident that somewhere
among the eight shelf-miles of records at the India Office
Library I would find what I needed to know – the precise
whereabouts on the Simla Mall of Lurgan's, or rather Jacob's,
'quaint little shop'. And if I failed to find it there, then there
was the huge photographic archive to explore. For surely
among the early photographs of Simla there would be one
of the shops on the Mall. And, if so, it was just possible that
one of these would bear the words A.M. JACOB, JEWELLER
AND CURIO DEALER, or something like it. After a lengthy
search, however, I was forced to admit defeat, for nowhere
could I find any reference to the shop, nor any glimpse of

it in the faded photographs of the Raj summer capital.
But I did discover one clue. I found that in addition to
living at Belvedere, on the outskirts of Simla, Jacob had at
one time occupied a smaller house, called Winscottie, which
stood on the same road, though rather closer to the town
centre. Indeed, for a while he appeared to occupy both houses
simultaneously. Was it possible, I wondered, that Winscottie
was where he had his shop? Not only was it more conveniently situated than Belvedere for this purpose, but it did,
strictly speaking, lie on the Mall. For contemporary maps of
Simla show that this thoroughfare extended far further than
most present-day visitors probably realise, looping round
behind Jakko, the great tree-clad hill which towers over
Simla, before returning to the town centre, a distance of
several miles in all. It was possible, though this is no more
than speculation, that when Jacob's business began to take
off, and he moved up the social scale, he transferred his
home from the modest Winscottie to the far grander and
more secluded Belvedere while maintaining the former
for his business activities. If so, then it was Winscottie
that Kipling had in mind when describing Lurgan Sahib's
shop.

I now set about trying to prove my theory, or at least to
find further evidence to support it. It was just conceivable,
I thought, that among the many volumes of memoirs left
by former Raj officials, most of whom would have visited
Simla at some time, there would be a reference to Jacob and
his celebrated shop which might reveal its whereabouts. I
therefore went to the library of the School of Oriental and

African Studies, part of London University, where I knew such memoirs lay on the shelves in considerable quantities. However, a morning spent thumbing through their indexes in the hope of finding an entry under the name of *Jacob, A.M.* yielded nothing. By now, though, it had become almost an obsession. I devoted hours to going through the stock of dealers selling old picture postcards of India, of which enormous quantities exist, including many of Simla. Again I hoped to find one showing Jacob's shop, whether at Winscottie or elsewhere on the Mall. Fortunately a hundred or so such postcard specialists bring their stock up to London every month, embracing every subject and country under the sun, which made my search considerably easier. Even so, though I came upon, and bought, many fascinating old postcards, I ran up against a blank wall so far as Jacob's shop was concerned.

One last hope now remained. I had noticed that two new histories of Simla had recently been published in India, both written by authors living in the town. The first to be published was Pamela Kanwar's *Imperial Simla*, which came out in 1990, and which devotes a page to Jacob. The second, published two years later, was Raja Bhasin's *Simla: The Summer Capital of British India*, which contains three pages on the mysterious Jacob. Neither author, I noted, refers to the whereabouts of his shop, though this did not necessarily mean that neither of them knew. It was a long shot, especially in view of the uncertainties of the Indian mail, but I decided to write to them both and hope that one or other would come up with the answer. In the meantime, leaving this particular piece of the jigsaw on one side, I would carry on trying to figure out *Kim*'s remaining mysteries.

*

When Mahbub Ali reached Simla, determined to have it out with Colonel Creighton over Kim, he at once made his way to Lurgan Sahib's shop, where he knew the secret service chief to be. Here Creighton was examining a collection of Tibetan ghost-daggers, used ritually for stabbing demons and other evil spirits. He now found himself confronted by an 'openly mutinous' Mahbub, who insisted bluntly: 'The pony is made – finished – mouthed and paced, Sahib! From now on, day by day, he will lose his manners if he is kept at tricks. Drop the rein on his back and let him go. We need him.' Taken aback by this, Creighton protested that Kim was still only a boy of sixteen. But the Afghan brushed aside this European concept of maturity, declaring: 'When I was fifteen, I had shot my man and begot my man, Sahib.' Creighton looked to Lurgan for support, but in vain. '*I* should have used him long ago,' Lurgan replied. 'The younger the better ... I think you waste him now.' He proposed that Kim should be sent to the south, where one of Creighton's men engaged on a secret mission had been found murdered while posing as an Arab trader. The colonel vetoed this as too dangerous, adding that 'E23 has that in hand'. But he finally agreed that Kim should be removed from St Xavier's, the school being officially told that an unexpected vacancy had arisen for 'an assistant chain-man in the Canal Department'.

In fact, it was further agreed that for the first six months Kim should be allowed to travel the Road, thereby gaining in confidence and experience, while at the same time perfecting his disguise as an itinerant native physician. Mahbub Ali suggested that during this probationary period Kim should 'run' with the lama, using the Tibetan's quest for the River of the Arrow as a cover. 'He is fond of the old man,' the Afghan explained, adding that Kim could usefully practise 'his paces by the rosary' during their search. Creighton then asked him how much he knew about the lama. 'He is quite mad,' Mahbub told him, 'but a peaceful man.' Both he and the Babu knew him. 'We have watched him for three years. Red Lamas are not so common in Hind that one loses track.'

The news that he was to leave St Xavier's forthwith was officially broken to Kim by his headmaster, who also gave him some advice on how to conduct his life. In my first edition of *Kim*, I notice that he refers to Kim as being seventeen. Yet only a few days earlier Creighton speaks of him as 'not more than sixteen'. The seventeen is clearly a slip by either Kipling or the compositor, for it is corrected to sixteen in subsequent editions, although reprints following the first-edition text continue, nearly a century later, to perpetuate the error. Not surprisingly, for they were Kipling's publishers, the Macmillan editions appear to have got it right. So have the Penguin and Pan paperback editions. But the Oxford University Press and Wordsworth paperbacks, which sell in large numbers, repeat the error, as do a number of other editions. Apart from adding a whole year to the young hero's age, thereby changing the reader's conception of him, this might not matter too much. However, together with an earlier misconception, the error over his age has caused at least one Kipling scholar to get wrong by several years the period over which the narrative takes place.

Kim, in fact, was already aware that he was leaving school for the Road, having the previous day received a letter from Mahbub Ali telling him of Colonel Creighton's decision, and arranging a rendezvous between Kim, the Babu and himself the following afternoon at a house whose very name, Kipling tells us, 'would have crisped the Principal's hair with horror'. Here, in a darkened upper room, there took place a bizarre scene which allowed Kipling to indulge once more his fascination with the occult and the supernatural, especially of the oriental kind. For at the back of a tobacco-shop, at the top of a flight of filthy stairs, there lived a gruesome-looking woman called Huneefa, who practised, among other strange things, as a witch. They found her, clad in heavy native jewellery which sounded 'like the clashing of copper pots' whenever she moved, lying on some dirty cushions sucking at a hookah, or oriental water-pipe.

Huneefa, Mahbub explained to Kim, possessed the recipe of a secret dye for darkening the skin which was extremely long-lasting, and which would see out his six months on the Road with the lama. Kim was made to strip to the waist, revealing his white European skin. As she advanced towards him clutching a pewter bowl in her bejewelled hand, Kim suddenly realised that she was blind. Then a match flickered in the gloom and the room was filled with incense – 'heavy, aromatic, and stupefying' – as Huneefa explained that the darkening of Kim's skin was only part of the protection she was able to give him on the Road. As she worked the dye into his skin, she began to moan and to whisper strange invocations in Kim's ear. At that point he lost consciousness, while Huneefa – 'in some sort of drugged ecstasy' – called upon devil after devil, by name, not to harm him. Finally, frothing at the mouth, she collapsed exhausted and motionless beside Kim.

When Kim finally awoke, after what seemed like 'a sleep of a thousand years', Mahbub Ali had gone, leaving Huneefa snoring heavily in a corner and the Babu scribbling earnestly into a notebook all he could remember of what he had just seen. For ethnology was his private passion, and these weird manifestations of native witchcraft were quite unlike anything he had ever witnessed before. Indeed, despite professing – as an MA of Calcutta University – not to believe in such mumbo-jumbo, but merely to study it, he had found the whole episode distinctly alarming. He knew, however, that what he had just seen would provide him with unusually interesting material for a learned article on outlandish cults and religions, which were his special subject. For he regularly bombarded scientific journals in London and elsewhere with monographs on such matters, hoping one day for publication, and eventually perhaps an invitation to put the letters FRS – Fellow of the Royal Society – after his name. Curiously, as it happened, this was an ambition shared by Colonel Creighton, his head of department, who was also given to submitting learned articles to scientific journals. It was no surprise to me to discover, therefore, that Colonel Montgomerie – whom I believe to be Kipling's inspiration for Colonel Creighton – was elected a Fellow of the Royal Society in 1872 for his scientific work in India.

PHILOSOPHICAL
TRANSACTIONS
OF THE
ROYAL SOCIETY
OF
LONDON
(A)
FOR THE YEAR MDCCCLXXXVIII.
VOL. 179.

LONDON:
PRINTED BY HARRISON AND SONS, ST MARTIN'S LANE, W.C.,
Printers in Ordinary to Her Majesty.
MCCCLXXXIX

Quite why the hard-bitten Mahbub Ali, that firm believer in the law of the gun, should think that Huneefa's macabre spells and drugs could protect Kim from the evils of the Road, is somewhat puzzling, not to say out of character. Certainly the Babu considered it odd. 'It was', he explained to Kim apologetically, 'Mahbub's desire.' The Afghan, he added disdainfully, was 'highly obsolete' in believing in such things. Even so, as they prepared to leave, he was careful to avoid stepping on the sleeping witch's shadow.

The Babu had brought with him from Lurgan Sahib in Simla some clothes for Kim – those that would be worn by a *chela* to a Tibetan lama. Kim, his skin now as dark as any hillman's, slipped into these, and together they set out for the railway station. It was on the way there that the Babu let Kim into one of the 'strictly unofficial' secrets of what he called 'our Department'. It was one, he told Kim proudly, that he himself had introduced to the Great Game. So unofficial was it, in fact, that even Colonel Creighton did not know about it. 'He is European,' the Babu added by way of explanation, forgetting perhaps that so too was the swarthy youngster strutting barefoot in the dust beside him.

Kim, the Babu revealed, would from now on enjoy the protection of a native secret society called the *Sat Bhai*, or Seven Brothers. It was thought to be extinct, but he had discovered during his ethnological work that it still flourished. Invoking its name, he explained, might well save Kim's life one day if he found himself in 'a dam'-tight place'. He himself, he told Kim, had been 'in dam'-tight places more than hairs on my head'. Were Kim to find himself in a tight spot he should call out to those who threatened him: 'I am Son of the Charm.' The *Sat Bhai*, he added, 'has many members, and perhaps before they jolly-well-cut-your-throat they may give you just a chance . . . And moreover, these foolish natives – if they are not too excited – they always stop to think before they kill a man who says he belongs to any specific organisation.' At the same time, were he called upon by a Son of the Charm for help he must do everything in his power to protect him.

But that was not all. On awakening from his drugged sleep Kim had found, suspended around his neck on a plaited copper wire, a tiny amulet made of cheap silver and black enamel. Explaining its purpose, the Babu told him that it

was a sort of identity tag to enable those who played the Great Game to recognise one another if they had never met before or were in disguise. The amulets were made 'onlee for us' by Huneefa herself, who inserted in each one a scrap of paper bearing the names of saints. To be absolutely certain that no one else could obtain one, a tiny piece of turquoise was wrapped in Huneefa's list of saints by Lurgan Sahib (who, not being a real English sahib, was allowed to know certain things kept from Colonel Creighton).

The Babu also explained to Kim how to make use of special secret words when conversing with individuals met on the Road to discover whether they were Sons of the Charm. For very likely they would be heavily disguised if engaged in secret service work. One day, said the Babu, he himself might appear to Kim as a Ladakhi trader. 'You would not know me at all . . . I bet you,' he added. But these code words would allow them to identify themselves and make contact, even among foes or strangers. If further proof were needed, then the amulet containing the turquoise fragment could be produced. 'It is', the Babu assured Kim, 'verree easy.' Then, with a cheerful 'Goodbye, my dear fellow,' he vanished into the crowds outside Lucknow railway station.

Something about the Sons of the Charm, with their elaborate and mysterious rituals and secret recognition signs, struck me as rather familiar. And yet, if my more learned Indian friends were to be believed, there never was a secret society in India called the *Sat Bhai*. 'It is a pure Kipling invention,' insisted one. Then it dawned on me. At the age of twenty, while still below the minimum age, Kipling became a Freemason, joining one of five lodges which existed in Lahore. For Freemasonry was widespread throughout British India, and was in fact the only forum where intelligent and successful men of all races could meet and talk. Kipling tells us that he was entered by a Hindu, passed by a Muslim and raised by an Englishman, in a lodge which also included Jews and other minorities.

Allusions as well as direct references to Freemasonry appear in many of Kipling's works, with a dozen or more in *Kim* alone. In *Puck of Pook's Hill*, moreover, he draws an analogy between ancient Mithraism – worship of the Indo-Iranian sun-god – and Freemasonry. It is not too far-fetched, therefore, to see Freemasonry, with its jealously guarded rituals, as the inspiration for the Babu's secret club within a club.

Indeed, Kipling scholars have often pointed out his preoccupation with élite groups of like-minded men, dedicated to a common task or cause, from which all others are excluded. This Kiplingesque brand of élitism, it must be said, had nothing whatever to do with rank, race or social position. After all, Kim's opium-befuddled father, although only an NCO, had been a Mason, while both Colonel Creighton and the Babu secretly longed to be invited to become Fellows of the Royal Society, that ultimate in scientific recognition.

And before we leave the subject of Freemasonry, perhaps I should add that 'the big blue and white Jadoo-Gher – the Magic House', as Kipling calls Lahore's old Masonic temple, still stands today. It is, however, no longer a meeting-place for Masons, where Muslims, Hindus, Jews and Europeans could conjoin on equal terms. Gone for ever is the magnificent carved-wood furniture of Kipling's day, the valuable library and the fine stained-glass window portraying Solomon. For not all governments, particularly Islamic ones, welcome Freemasonry, and the 'Magic House' was long ago sequestrated by the authorities for their own secular use. (All that the Freemasons' London headquarters say of the lodge's fate is that, in common with others in Muslim countries, it is 'in abeyance'.)

*

Preoccupied by the strange goings-on at Huneefa's house, I had momentarily forgotten about my search for Jacob's shop. It was with some excitement, therefore, that one morning in London I received a letter bearing a Simla postmark. Ripping it open, I was delighted to find that it was from Raja Bhasin, one of the two authors of recent books on Simla to whom I had written in the hope of finally solving the shop's mystery. It was a charming letter, but any hopes I might have had of a quick solution to my quest were swiftly dashed. 'I really wish', he began, 'that I could categorically say that Jacob had a shop on the Mall, and that this was it . . .' But although he himself lived in Simla, he had not been able to discover for certain where the shop had been. 'The popular notion', he added, was that it was located at Hamilton House, towards the eastern end of the main stretch of shops looking down on the Lower Bazaar from the Mall. However, he had not been able to find any evidence to substantiate this.

During my own investigations in Simla, I too had been given this spot, among several other possibilities, as the original site of Jacob's shop. In London I had already explored the likelihood of this. Old Simla directories at the India Office Library showed Hamilton & Co., after whom the building was named, to be a long-standing firm of jewellers, though of the christening bowl and engagement ring variety. Indeed, they were flourishing at precisely the same time as Jacob, so these premises could not possibly have been his curio shop. Also Hamilton & Co. appeared to back on to the slopes of Jakko, which meant that their rear veranda would have looked upwards, rather than 'into their neighbours' chimney-pots, as is the custom of Simla'.

Unless positive evidence to the contrary was forthcoming, I was beginning to suspect that the Hamilton House theory had arisen simply because they, too, happened to be jewellers, leading local people subsequently to jump to conclusions.

There is, however, one flaw in this argument. In her Raj memoirs the novelist M. M. Kaye, who was herself born in Simla, also places Jacob's shop in that part of the Mall. Yet this can only have been hearsay, for she was not born until 1908, when her parents moved to Simla, so neither she nor they could have known the shop at first hand, since by then Jacob was living in Bombay. She adds, interestingly, that her father bought two small oriental carpets, subsequently owned by herself, which were 'part of Jacob's stock'. Clearly, though, these were not purchased from the mysterious Jacob himself. She wrote this in her eighties, and admitted that her memory was 'beginning to fail'. Nonetheless, she insists that when she returned to Simla in the 1960s the shop said to have been Jacob's was still there on the Mall.

Despite all this, I still had hopes that Pamela Kanwar, the other Simla historian to whom I had written, might come up with the definitive solution, having chanced upon it perhaps when exploring the summer capital's municipal archives, of which she makes extensive use in her book, with its page on Jacob, and in an earlier doctoral thesis. I now found myself waiting eagerly for every mail, my eyes skinned for a letter bearing a Simla postmark. It was not long in coming, and I tore it open like a man possessed. In fact, it was written from Delhi, for it transpired that Dr Kanwar had moved there from Simla since writing her book. It was an utterly charming letter, but any hopes I might have entertained that it would pinpoint for me the precise whereabouts on the Mall of Jacob's elusive shop proved vain. She had gone carefully through all her Simla notes, she explained, but 'could not find anything definitive'. However, she would be returning to Simla before very long for further work on the archives there, and most kindly promised to let me know if she came upon the answer. This was an extraordinarily generous gesture, as I had seriously considered making a special trip myself to explore those same archives.

In spite of Edward Buck's assertion about the shop, and M. M. Kaye's memory of where it was said to have stood, the fact that two serious historians living on the spot were unable to locate it in what is really a very small town now made me begin to wonder whether it ever stood among the shops on the Mall, save in hearsay or as a piece of tourist folklore. Unless Dr Kanwar were to come up with evidence to the contrary, the only explanation which seemed to fit was that Jacob's mysterious establishment was a shop-within-a-house, meaning Winscottie, since this, technically speaking, stood on the Mall. We may never know for certain, the final truth being lost to history, like so much else concerning this extraordinary individual.

Among a number of false trails I had followed during my quest, both in Simla and in London, was that of Imre Schwaiger, 'whose establishment in Simla', Buck tells us, 'used to be one of the main attractions on the Mall'. According to Buck, who was after all living there at the time, Schwaiger 'succeeded' Jacob as the hill-station's leading dealer in oriental treasures in 1904. Buck does not, however, say that he took over Jacob's premises, and as he refers to both shops he would surely have said so if they were one and the same. Another contemporary account also bears out this view.

Perhaps because Schwaiger's establishment stood more or less opposite Hamilton & Co., this has contributed to the confusion of the present day. And two points that Jacob and Schwaiger had in common – both foreigners and both curio dealers – probably helped to blur their identities once there was no one left who actually remembered them.

So much then for A. M. Jacob, immortalised by Kipling in the compellingly sinister figure of Lurgan Sahib. In fact, all along it has been Lurgan Sahib's weird shop that we have really been hoping to discover on the Simla Mall, on the dubious assumption that the fictional one was modelled by Kipling, down to its very location, on the real-life one belonging to Jacob. Yet, on reflection, it seems unlikely that Kipling would have hijacked Jacob in his entirety, if only out of common decency. For at the time *Kim* was being written, the unfortunate Jacob was still living in Simla, desperately trying to fight off bankruptcy and salvage his reputation. As it was, Kipling borrowed the more sensational aspects of his character, together with the outlandish atmosphere and artefacts of his shop, and transferred these to an establishment somewhere on the Mall, whose precise location was known only to himself. Fans of *Kim*, myself included, have been trying to find it ever since. Maybe the answer would be for someone to open a small antique shop on the Mall, cram it with Tibetan and other exotic treasures, and call it 'Lurgan Sahib's Original Oriental Curio Shop'. If life in Britain becomes too unbearable, I might even consider it myself.

\*

Perhaps Jacob, wherever he now is, did not appreciate my probing into his private affairs, let alone my last, somewhat facetious suggestion, and decided – his occult powers undiminished by death – to make his displeasure known. For it was while I was on my way to the India Office Library and Records to search for his will that I discovered to my dismay that I had lost my entire set of notes for the remainder of this book. These, jotted down on the back of index cards, together with cuttings from Indian newspapers, I kept in a battered and heavily annotated copy of *Kim*, which I took everywhere with me. Suddenly I found that the book and my notes were neither in my jacket pocket, where I sometimes kept them for quick access when travelling, nor in my briefcase. A hurried search of my home, and a careful retracing of my footsteps earlier that morning, including visits to lost-property offices, yielded nothing. My notes and annotations, which represented weeks, if not months, of work, had simply vanished, as though by levitation, and it took me several days to reconcile myself to the fact that I was not going to see them again. I even considered abandoning the book.

Although I cannot say I seriously believe in messages or warnings from beyond the grave, this was not the only thing that happened while I was searching for Jacob's will. Just as I entered the reading room to commence my research, the alarm bells all started to ring, and we had to evacuate the building for forty minutes. In fact, I never found any trace of his will (which would have been there if anywhere) or even an inventory of his possessions, and I believe that he died intestate and almost destitute. Perhaps it was now time to lay off Jacob before something far worse befell me! I therefore turned my attention to Kim, who was, it may be recalled, about to leave Lucknow by train for Benares. There he was eagerly looking forward to a reunion with his old friend the lama, and to making plans – with Colonel Creighton's secret blessing – to continue their search together for the River of the Arrow.

# 12

# *Enter the Russians*

WHEN KIM SET out from Lucknow for Benares, he left behind a city which, in Raj lore at least, symbolised the ultimate in British heroism and self-sacrifice. The successful though bloody defence of the Lucknow Residency in 1857 during the murderous heat of summer was to become one of the great epics of the Indian Mutiny. Gradually reduced to ruins during the long bombardment by the mutineers, what little remained of this once handsome building is now preserved exactly as it was when the siege was finally lifted. Ever since, it has served as a shrine to the memory of the 2,000 men, women and children who perished there, and who today are buried close by.

On the lawn in front of the Residency stands a marble runic cross, erected to commemorate the valiant death of Sir Henry Lawrence, the hero of the siege, and the many other 'brave men' who fell during the five-month-long ordeal. In the event of any misfortune befalling Lord Canning, the Governor-General of India, Lawrence had already been chosen to succeed him. His grave, by the ruins of the Residency church, bears the epitaph which he requested as he lay dying. It reads simply: 'Here lies Henry Lawrence, who tried to do his duty.' In the shattered entrance to the Residency, a marble plaque tells the story of its defence. Included in it are Canning's celebrated words: 'There does not stand recorded in the annals of war an achievement more heroic.'

Throughout the siege, from a tower on one corner of the Residency, a Union Jack had fluttered defiantly around the clock. Ever afterwards, in commemoration of this, a Union Jack was flown day and night from that same tower, never once being lowered, except for replacement. It was a singular honour, for every other Union Jack right across the British Empire was hauled down ceremoniously at sunset, usually to the plangent notes of the Last Post. Only on August 15, 1947, when the British left India for good, was the Union Jack on the Residency finally lowered. And then, to make sure that no other flag would ever fly from it again, a sapper from the Royal Engineers climbed up into the tower and with an axe solemnly cut through the historic flagstaff, while another cemented in the hole that this left.

Nowadays few British visitors come to Lucknow to pay homage to the Residency's defenders, or wander among the memorial plaques and graves so scrupulously maintained and protected by the Indian authorities. For today there is little interest in the Mutiny, or the Indian War of Independence as many Indians prefer to call it, and anyway the city lies somewhat off the regular tourist beat. Nonetheless, unde-terred by this and proud of their city's dramatic past, the municipal authorities have recently launched a new initiative to attract visitors to Lucknow, especially British ones, who can now stay in air-conditioned luxury in one of India's finest hotels. With an awareness of history, moreover, they have invited Cox and Kings, a British travel agency which has been bringing people to India since 1758, a whole century before the Mutiny, to help them reawaken interest in Luck-now's rich heritage and Raj connections. Originally founded to arrange the outward and homeward journeys of East India Company officials and their families, Cox and Kings is the oldest travel agency in the world. Indeed, it would almost certainly have organised the voyage to India of the young Rudyard Kipling when, in 1882, he went out to join the staff of the *Civil and Military Gazette* in Lahore.

In Kipling's day, the horrors of the Indian Mutiny were still fresh in many people's minds, for it had taken place only twenty-five years previously. Fears of a second such uprising were an ever-present nightmare to those responsible for the defence of India and the safety of its white population. These fears were intensified during both world wars. In the first, the Germans and the Turks together tried to set British India ablaze from within by igniting an explosive cocktail of religious and nationalist sensibilities, while in the second the Japanese also attempted to harness Indian disaffection to their war effort. Both failed. Then, after some ninety years of disturbed nights, such fears of a second Indian Mutiny ended with the coming of independence. However, the dreadful religious bloodbath which followed showed what it might have been like had Colonel Creighton's real-life colleagues been less vigilant.

Today the Allahabad *Pioneer*, which Kipling joined in 1887, has transferred its base of operations to Lucknow. Intrigued to see how it had changed since his day, I bought a copy and began to turn the pages. Suddenly my eye fell on a chilling story – 'the most sensational crime', the *Pioneer* called it, 'in Lucknow's recent history'. Stalking the streets of Lucknow was a serial killer of boys of around Kim's age. To date he had strangled and mutilated five such youngsters, dumping their corpses in back streets between La Martinière school and the railway station. For the school staff, responsible for the safety of so many teenage boys, it must have been a nightmare. I never discovered whether the killer was eventually caught, but I could not help thinking of Kim as I read the gruesome details – that is until I remembered the pearl-handled revolver which Mahbub Ali had given him and which he kept next to his skin now that he had shed his school uniform for the last time.

\*

On leaving the train at Benares – today called Varanasi – Kim made straight for the Temple of the Tirthankars, where he knew the lama to be staying. This, Kipling tells us, lay 'about a mile outside the city, near Sarnath' – a town as sacred to Buddhists and to Tirthankars, or Jains, as Benares is to Hindus. I had hoped to pinpoint the precise whereabouts of this particular temple where the lama had, on and off, spent the previous three years waiting patiently for Kim to finish his education as a learned sahib before returning to the Search. However, Kipling's description of its location makes this difficult, if not impossible, for Sarnath lies six miles or more north of Benares. How, therefore, could the temple have stood 'about a mile outside' Benares and at the same time be 'near Sarnath'? In Kipling's day – and we know that he first visited Benares in 1887 to report on the new bridge carrying the Grand Trunk Road over the sacred River Ganges – both Benares and Sarnath would have been considerably smaller, and their limits therefore even further apart. There is at least one Jain temple in Benares, and another in the middle of Sarnath. But, irrespective of this, there could not really be anything, temple or otherwise, at the ambiguous location Kipling gives us. My own guess is that he made it up, never dreaming that some busybody like myself, a whole century later, would try to find it.

Kim's reunion with the old Tibetan, like so many moments in their relationship, is tenderly described by Kipling, who devotes several pages to it. After Kim has thanked his unlikely benefactor for saving him from three years in an army orphanage, and sending him instead to one of the most expensive schools in India, the lama leads him into the temple's sunlit courtyard. Then, peering keenly at his *chela* through narrow eyes, he declares: 'So! It is no longer a child, but a man, ripened in wisdom,' adding, 'I did well – I did well when I gave thee up to the armed men on that black night.' After that they fell to reminiscing about how they had first met by Zam-Zammah, outside the 'Wonder

House', and all that had happened to them since. Finally they agreed that, until it was time for Kim to begin working 'as a scribe' for Colonel Creighton, they would take the Road together and continue their Search for the River of the Arrow. First they would go north, via Delhi, to Saharunpore, where they knew that the Sahiba – the widow from Kulu – would welcome them at her farmhouse among the fruit-trees. That night, Kipling tells us, Kim fell asleep at the foot of the tiny, carved wooden altar in the lama's cell, and 'dreamed in Hindustani, with never an English word'.

They shared their railway compartment next day with a Punjabi peasant farmer whose young son Kim had cured of fever, using the little medicine chest the Babu had given him. It was his first test as a native doctor, but he remembered what Lurgan Sahib had taught him about drugs, and also the treatment he himself had received for malaria in the sanatorium at St Xavier's. Happily it worked, and the farmer insisted on travelling with them, hailing Kim as a 'worker of miracles'. While the lama clicked his prayer-beads and drowsed away the long hot journey, Kim gazed excitedly out at the shimmering landscape, imagining the adventures to come. Whenever a peasant entered the compartment, Kim would engage him in chit-chat, explaining why the inspector punched a great hole in the *tikkut* he had just paid so much for, and generally revelling in his newly found self-importance as healer and sage.

On Indian trains in those days all barriers of caste and religion were set aside for the duration of the journey, and personal confidences, not to mention provisions, were freely shared between strangers. Alas, such trust no longer exists on the 'te-rain'. The 'Crime and Railways Cell' of the Delhi Police (watchword: 'With You, For You, Always') places regular advertisements in the newspapers warning travellers never to accept food or drink from strangers. 'Sometimes', they explain, 'these will be drugged to send you to sleep.' By the time you wake up, that passenger who so kindly shared his lunch with you 'may be hundreds of miles away', together with your valuables. They illustrate their warning with a melodramatically posed photograph of an elderly, trusting passenger accepting a succulent delicacy from a suave, smirking individual with a villainous-looking moustache. To be quite safe, they suggest, you should pad-lock your luggage to your seat with a chain.

Without his vigilant, bazaar-educated *chela*, the totally trusting lama would not, it appears, have survived two minutes in today's India. And yet, as holy men, he and Kim would nowadays be allowed to travel on the 'te-rain' free – or so I read somewhere. For tales about Indian Railways, both true and untrue, are legion. One I like is about dogs on trains. In 1902, the year after *Kim* was published, an American woman – Eliza Scidmore – touring India by rail noticed and jotted down this warning to dog-owners who wished to take their pet, or pets, with them. 'Passengers', it declared, 'will not be allowed to take any dog into a passenger carriage, except with the permission of the Station Master at the starting station, and also with the consent of their fellow passengers, and then only on payment of a double fare for each dog, subject to the condition that it shall be

removed if subsequently objected to, no refund being given.'
The number of dogs thus travelling, it added, 'must not
exceed three'. The ordinance was signed by 'His Excellency
the Governor-General in Council'. Fortunately, as it happened, Kim and the lama were not travelling with a dog –
or, worse, three. Yet that would have been child's play compared with what happened to them next.

Suddenly, just as they were pulling out of Somna Road
station, some sixty miles short of Delhi, the torpor which
until then had pervaded the journey was abruptly disturbed.
For there tumbled into their compartment a small, dishev-
elled figure who – thanks to Lurgan Sahib's training, and
from his turban – Kim guessed to be a Mahratta from south-
west India. 'His face', wrote Kipling, 'was cut', his clothes
were badly torn, and one of his legs was bandaged. He
apologised for his state, explaining that he had been thrown
from a country cart in which he was travelling when it
overturned. Kim's highly developed powers of observation,
however, told him that the man was lying, for his clean cuts
were not consistent with falling from a cart. Nor would a
mere road accident have cast a man 'into such extremity of
terror', for Kim noticed that his hands were shaking as he
straightened his torn clothing.

But that was not all that Kim noticed. Suddenly he caught
sight of a small amulet suspended from the man's neck. To
his utter astonishment he saw that it was fashioned from
silver and black enamel, and hung on a loop of plaited copper
wire. It was exactly like the one the Babu had given him –
the identity tag of the Great Game, by means of which the

players could always recognise one another. Discreetly he drew out his own so that the newcomer could see it. There quickly followed an exchange of the secret passwords that the Babu had taught him, and Kim then knew that this injured man was a Son of the Charm, and badly in need of his help. Turning to the others in the compartment – the lama was still asleep – and adopting the air of a native physician, he explained that he was now going to examine the man's injuries. Then, leaning forward so that he could not be overheard, he whispered: 'Tell thy tale swiftly, brother, while I say a charm', and began to mumble some mystical words he had learned from Lurgan Sahib.

Agent E23 – as he turned out to be – told Kim that Colonel Creighton had sent him to an independent state in the south to complete the mission of another agent, who had been murdered while disguised as an Arab trader by those he was spying on. What Creighton was anxious to get his hands on was a particularly incriminating letter, thought to implicate Constantinople, and this E23 had managed to acquire, only to discover that its owners had got wind of this and had put a heavy price on his head. He had immediately hidden the letter, intending to return for it once the hue and cry had died down. 'I wished the credit of it all,' he explained to Kim, who understood and nodded sympathetically. The hunt for E23 had intensified, however, his pursuers accusing him of murder and even bribing the local police to hand him over to them if they caught him.

But surely, said Kim, the Indian government would protect him from such evildoers. 'We of the Game are beyond protection,' E23 reminded him. 'If we die, we die. Our names are blotted from the book. That is all.' He explained how he had acquired his injuries. Shortly before getting on the train he had been attacked as he lay hiding in a ditch, weak from fever and from not having eaten for two days. Clearly his assailant was looking for the missing letter, for he ran off after forcibly searching him and finding he did not have it. But his pursuers now knew that he was on the train, and at Delhi the police would be waiting to arrest him on the trumped-up murder charge. His powerful enemies in the south not only had witnesses prepared to swear that they had seen him commit the crime, but also a real corpse. He could see no way of escape, for he would easily be recognisable from his injuries when the police boarded the train.

Kim was determined at all costs to save his fellow-agent from the imminent danger awaiting him. Aware that he did not have a moment to spare, for very shortly they would be arriving in Delhi, he feverishly set about the plan he had worked out. First he announced importantly, for all to hear, that he had completed his examination of the injured man, and that he now proposed to heal him. This, he explained, would depend on the patient performing some suitable act of penance. For the next few days, therefore, he would have to follow the calling of a *baraigi*, or wandering ascetic, and live by begging. Kim next began to transform E23 from a Mahratta trader into a religious mendicant, trying hard to remember all that Lurgan Sahib had taught him about the art of disguise. Just how he achieved this is best discovered from the pages of *Kim*, where it is brilliantly told. The disguise was completed in the nick of time, as their train steamed into Delhi. 'In place of the tremulous, shrinking trader,' Kipling tells us, 'there lolled against the corner an all but naked, ash-smeared, ocre-barred, dusty-haired Saddhu, his swollen eyes – opium takes quick effect on an empty stomach – luminous with insolence and bestial lust, his legs crossed under him, Kim's brown rosary round his neck . . .'

The police, who were waiting on the platform, now poured on to the train, led by a perspiring young British officer. 'Behind them, inconspicuous as a cat,' Kim observed 'a small fat person who looked like a lawyer's tout.' Clearly this was the evil genius, representing his masters in the south, who had hoodwinked the authorities in Delhi into believing the false murder charge. When the police posse reached the compartment where E23 sat with his companions, studiously counting his prayer-beads, the Englishman called out derisively 'Nothing here but a parcel of holy-bolies.' To the intense relief of E23 and Kim – the lama and the Punjabi farmer having little, if any, idea of what was really going on – they continued on down the train. But though he was now out of immediate danger, E23's vexations were not yet over. How, he asked Kim, was he to alert Creighton to the precise spot where he had hidden the vital letter? Dressed as he was, he could hardly make his way to the telegraph office to send Creighton a wire without drawing considerable attention to himself.

But help, if unexpected, was at hand. Walking through the train some distance behind the main police party was another sahib, whose uniform marked him out as District Superintendent of Police. Seeing him, E23 quickly rose on the pretext of getting himself some water, but then deliberately – or so it appeared to Kim – bumped into the Englishman. Angry words were exchanged, with E23 directing at the sahib 'a stream of the filthiest abuse'. To add further insult, E23 then held out his ticket, as though mistaking the superintendent for a railway inspector. More angry words followed. Then, apparently realising his error, E23 began to fawn upon the Englishman and apologise to him. All this, it transpired, was a deliberate charade, as E23 subsequently explained to Kim. The angry police officer was none other than Strickland Sahib, a leading player in the Great Game, who crops up in a number of Kipling's short stories, notably in 'Miss Youghal's *Sais*'. A master of disguise when investigating evil-doing, he believed that a policeman in India should 'try to know as much about the natives as the natives themselves', while legend had it that he could make himself invisible. There are obvious shades of Jacob here, though the most likely model for Strickland is John Paul Warburton, a real-life District Superintendent of Police with a reputation akin to that attributed to Strickland by Kipling. But as Strickland plays only a passing role in *Kim*, I shall not pursue this further here.

Kim, meanwhile, had just had the chance to watch a Great Game professional in action. For behind the smokescreen of angry words and abuse, E23 had been able to describe to Strickland – whom he had recognised as he boarded the train – where exactly he had hidden the letter, so that its recovery could be discreetly arranged. 'Strickland Sahib', E23 told Kim, 'has saved me from the present calamity, but I owe my life to thee.' Just why Strickland was at the railway station we do not discover, though perhaps that is simply part of the legend surrounding him. But two hours later, Kipling tells us, 'several telegrams had reached the angry minister of a southern state reporting that all trace of a somewhat bruised Mahratta had been lost'. Meanwhile E23 had left the train under the protective eye of Strickland, while the Punjabi farmer, having had as much as he could take of holy men, not to mention policemen, had gathered up his son and fled. Kim and the lama, with the compartment to themselves at last, now continued on their leisurely journey to Saharunpore.

\*

In Kipling's day, Saharunpore was a British railway colony surrounded by large, privately owned fruit farms, on one of which, as we know, lived the widow of Kulu with her daughter and son-in-law. Lockwood Kipling, writing in 1891, described the town as 'an Indian Crewe or Swindon', albeit on a smaller scale. In his now little-read masterpiece *Beast and Man in India* he tells the comical story of what happened when the British authorities decided to send into exile there a large number of sacred monkeys, who obviously could not be culled but who were becoming a serious nuisance in India's major cities. All other methods, hitherto, had failed. When one group of captives were caged and conveyed on bullock-carts into the wilds, many miles from town, these intelligent creatures had simply bounded home alongside the returning carts – 'and trooped in through the city gates with the air of a holiday party returning from a picnic'.

It was at last decided to consign several wagon-loads of these troublesome animals by train to Saharunpore. This was the nearest railhead to their final destination, the beautiful Himalayan foothills to the north (to which I, for one, would be only too happy to be exiled). Unfortunately, while being offloaded at Saharunpore, the monkeys made a mass-escape and stormed the railway workshops and engine-sheds, causing mayhem among the machinery. 'A large male', Kipling senior tells us, 'was seen pulling the point-levers of a siding', while his companions pilfered legs of mutton, corkscrews and other items, for which they could have had no possible use, from the inspection carriages in which some of the railway engineers lived. Nor were they easily driven out, though eventually most of them made their way to the town's many orchards and gardens. The owners of these, Lockwood recounts, 'being mainly Muhammadans with no respect for Hanuman [the monkey god], took measures of their own against the invasion'.

Today, when you drive north from Saharunpore into the hills, the whole place is running with monkeys, some sitting on the roadside idly watching the cars go by, others playing 'chicken', sprinting across the road right under your wheels. Perhaps these are the great-great-great-great-grandchildren of those who managed to escape the fruit-farmers' wrath, or of others whom the authorities did finally succeed in deporting. Anyway, with their comical, semi-human antics, they guarantee today's traveller plenty of amusement. Many Hindus – or so Lockwood Kipling tells us – believe that the English are descended from Hanuman, a conclusion with which Darwin could hardly have quarrelled.

*

When Kim and the lama left the train at Saharunpore, the morning dew still glistened on the bougainvillaea. The early morning, Kipling tells us, is a time when Saharunpore, named after a Muslim saint, is 'clean and well scented'. Alas, a century later, when I was there, a heavy pall of industrial smog hung over the town, once a favourite summer resort of the Mogul court. At Saharunpore one changes for Dehra Dun, where Colonel Montgomerie trained his 'pundits', and for the sleepy little hill-station of Mussoorie, but not much else – unless, that is, you are there for the annual Mango

Festival, for mangoes are Saharunpore's one remaining glory. Not surprisingly, perhaps, the town features in few modern guidebooks, and then meriting no more than a sentence or two.

Kim and the lama did not linger there, but headed out into the surrounding farmlands, passing through village after village, where Kim found that, despite his three years as a sahib, he had lost none of his old skill with a begging bowl. At midday they would rest, and at night they slept under the mango trees. Kim had suggested going straight to the Sahiba's farmhouse, but the lama vetoed this, saying that he wanted time to meditate, and to explain many things to Kim that St Xavier's could never teach him. Sometimes, at halts, he would draw out from beneath his robe the great folded sheet of paper on which he had portrayed the Wheel of Life and, unfolding it, would explain its mysteries to Kim. At other times he would tell him strange tales of Tibetan life – of holy cities fifteen thousand feet in the air, of avalanche-guarded cathedrals, of devil-dances, of the changing of monks and nuns into swine, of intrigues between monasteries, and of mysterious voices among the hills. Kim listened enthralled, for he had never before heard such tales, not even from Mahbub Ali or the Babu, let alone from the masters of St Xavier's.

'News travels quickly in India,' wrote Kipling of this land where little else does, and very soon the Sahiba had got to hear that her two old friends from the Grand Trunk Road were in the district. Before long, across the fields there appeared a white-whiskered retainer bearing a basket of fruit from her orchard and a pressing invitation to them to stay at her farmhouse. But the lama was in no hurry, for he had experienced her hospitality before, and despite her great generosity he found her exhausting and distracting with her unending flow of questions and requests for charms for her grandchildren. So it took them two days to walk the eleven miles to the farm, where they found her watching for them from an upper window.

It was while they were there that they learned of the presence of another guest – a Bengali physician, to whom the widow had turned in her ceaseless quest for cures. 'Who is the *hakim*, Maharanee?' Kim asked her, for he felt a sudden pang of jealousy at the thought of this newcomer usurping the lama's role as her medical and spiritual adviser. 'He travels about', she answered, 'vending preparations of great value. He has even papers, printed in Angrezi, telling what things he has done . . .' This was too much for Kim, who declared scornfully: 'Their stock-in-trade is a little coloured water and a very great shamelessness . . .' At that moment the newcomer appeared. 'I do not give *my* sick the mere ink in which a charm is written,' he said, 'but hot and rending drugs which descend and wrestle with the evil.' To which he added: 'I bear a degree from the great school at Calcutta . . .' At this, the Sahiba left them, declaring: 'Let the *hakim* and the young priest settle between them whether charms or medicine most avail.'

The moment she was out of earshot, the stranger turned to Kim and whispered: 'How do you do, Mister O'Hara? I am jolly glad to see you.' It was the Babu, or R17. Realising that he had been hoodwinked, Kim was furious. However, the Babu reminded him of his parting words at Lucknow – that the next time they met he might well be on a Great Game mission, and therefore in disguise. In fact, he had just returned from the south, where he had been sent to retrieve 'that beastly letter' which E23 had hidden. But why, Kim demanded to know, had he now come to the Sahiba's farm? 'I come', the Babu told him, 'to congratulate you on your extraordinary effeecient performance at Delhi', adding: 'I tell you we are all proud of you. It was verree neat and handy.' He had heard the full story from E23 himself, an old friend of his, and had in turn reported it to Lurgan Sahib, who was absolutely delighted. 'By Jove! It was splendid,' he declared. 'I come to tell you so.'

Thrilled though he was by such praise, Kim's oriental upbringing told him that 'babus do not travel far to retail compliments'. Why then was he here? 'Men do not come after one from Simla', he told the Babu, 'and change their dress for the sake of a few sweet words. I am not a child. Talk Hindi and let us get to the yolk of the egg . . . Why art thou here? Give a straight answer.' Protesting that Europeans who asked such direct questions were 'verree disconcerting', the Babu explained to Kim that there was never any respite in the Great Game. 'When every one is dead', he said, 'the Great Game is finished. Not before.' Fresh trouble was already afoot on the frontier, with Russian agents busy among the tribesmen.

Three years back, he reminded Kim, 'when thou wast given the stallion's pedigree by Mahbub Ali', a conspiracy between five northern kings had been crushed by a swift show of military might. Afterwards two of the kings – those of 'Hilas and Bunar' – had undertaken to guard the northern passes 'for a price', though for much less than it would have cost the British to station their own troops there. They had also agreed, at Indian government expense, to build roads in the mountains which could be used to rush troops up to the frontier in an emergency. The Babu himself had been sent to the north to keep an eye on things, first 'selling tea in Leh', and then as paymaster to the coolies working on the new roads. It was then that he had realised that there was treachery afoot. 'I sent word many times that these two kings were sold to the north,' he told Kim, adding that 'Mahbub Ali, who was yet further north, amply confirmed it.' He had also reported that the very roads for which he was paying out British money to the diggers 'were being made for the feet of strangers and enemies'. And by that he meant the Russians. Yet nothing was done about it.

The next thing that happened, the Babu continued, was that two strangers had crossed the passes from the north under the pretence of a shooting expedition. 'They bear guns,' he said, 'but they bear also chains and levels and compasses.' The two men had been well received by the kings of Hilas and Bunar, to whom they had made 'great promises' in the name of the Tsar. They were at that very moment exploring and mapping the valleys and passes, noting carefully: 'Here is a place to build a breastwork. Here can ye pitch a fort. Here can ye hold the road against an army.' Yet the Indian government continued to do nothing about it, even when the three other kings, 'who were *not* paid for guarding the passes, tell them by runner of the bad faith of Bunar and Hilas'. Only now, when all the evil was done, did the order come to him: 'Go north and see what those strangers do.' The Babu explained that he was planning to track the two men down and try to attach himself to them as an interpreter, or in some other capacity.

He now came to the point – the reason for his being at the farmhouse. He was, he confessed, 'a fearful man', and was worried about what these two spies might do to him if they discovered what he was up to. 'They are Russians,' he told Kim, 'and highly unscrupulous people. I – I do not want to consort with them without a witness.' If Kim had no pressing engagement with the lama, would he consider shadowing him as he went northwards in search of the bogus sportsmen? He had acquired a 'great opeenion' of Kim since hearing at first hand from E23 how he had saved his life. 'I do not suppose these two gentlemen will torture me,' he said, 'but I like to provide for possible contingency with European assistance.' Who better, in a 'dam'-tight place', than Kim?

Such flattery, plus the prospect of further Great Game adventures, was irresistible to Kim. The lama, moreover, would be only too relieved to escape from the Sahiba's some-what suffocating hospitality, even if he had no idea of what really lay behind their journey. The fact that they would be heading into his cool and beloved hills, of which he had spoken so often to Kim, meant that he would need little persuading. And so it was agreed between Kim and the Babu that he would set out on the morrow, while they would leave the next morning, following closely in his footsteps.

From now on the rumbustious character of the Babu plays an increasingly important role in *Kim*. Perhaps this is an appropriate moment – before we examine who the 'highly unscrupulous' Russians were – to stop and consider what real-life individual, if any, was Kipling's inspiration for this improbable hero whom Lurgan Sahib rated as one of the ten best players in the Great Game.

# 13

# *Who Was the Babu?*

MUCH OF THE drama of *Kim*, as we have seen, is inspired by the clandestine exploits of Colonel Montgomerie's pundits, out of which Kipling has created an all-seeing, India-wide secret service. 'The Great Game is so large', Mahbub Ali tells Kim, 'that one sees but little at a time.' And by giving his characters letters and numbers – C25, R17 and E23 – Kipling leads us to believe that Colonel Creighton controls dozens more of them throughout India and perhaps beyond. After all, if there is a C25, then presumably there is a C24, and likewise an R16, an E22, and so on. Again, if the Babu is one of the ten best players, then there must be numerous others who do not appear in *Kim*, but are busy elsewhere on the Great Game battlefield.

Montgomerie's pundits, for their part, were very few in number at any time, perhaps no more than half a dozen, although there were plenty of other Indians engaged in non-clandestine map-making for the Survey of India. The pundits were used only in hazardous areas like Afghanistan, Turkestan and Tibet, from which derives their fame. Virtually all of *Kim*, however, save for some hints about Mahbub Ali's exploits beyond the frontier, takes place within India's geographical boundaries, even if the enemy is from without. For this reason it would be wrong to say that Creighton's agents were *modelled* on the pundits, although they were clearly inspired by them. Who then was the inspiration for Hurree Chunder Mookerjee, alias the Babu, or R17?

The pundits, by and large, were highly intelligent and resourceful hillmen, both Hindu and Muslim, not to mention one Buddhist. At least one of them was a village schoolmaster, though for the most part they were men of little formal education. While Mahbub Ali and E23 might loosely fit this description, the Babu – the pedantic, widely read graduate of Calcutta University – clearly does not. But there was one real-life pundit who was different. Like Kipling's Babu he was a Bengali and a Hindu. Furthermore he was a graduate of Calcutta. Like the Babu, too, he had scholarly ambitions in the ethnographical and allied fields. In addition, rather more was known about him than the other pundits, for he wrote a book about one of his clandestine journeys into Tibet, posing as a Buddhist scholar, which was published in Calcutta in 1885, and later by John Murray in London, followed by a Russian translation. Almost certainly either Kipling or his father Lockwood would have known about him.

His name was Babu Sarat Chandra Das, and perhaps the

fictional Babu's middle name of *Chunder* is Kipling's way of acknowledging his debt to the real-life Bengali pundit. Born in 1849, at the age of twenty-five he was appointed head-master of a British-funded boarding school in the hill-station of Darjeeling for Tibetan and half-Tibetan boys living in northern India, some of whom were to be trained as surveyors against the hoped-for day when Tibet opened its frontiers to outsiders. It was his contact with these Tibetan boys and their families that fired Sarat Chandra Das's lifelong interest in Tibet, and resulted in his two journeys there, in 1879 and 1881. After his return from the second, the Tibetan authorities realised that they had been hoodwinked, and meted out the most terrible punishments, including execution by drowning, on those who had, in all innocence, welcomed him – a tragic episode in Anglo-Tibetan relations which I have described more fully in *Trespassers on the Roof of the World*.

Unlike the other pundits, who confined themselves to surveying particular routes – one produced the first modern map of Lhasa – Sarat Chandra Das brought back a wealth of political, economic and other intelligence, mostly confided to him by unsuspecting Tibetan officials. Subsequently he continued to live in Darjeeling – naming his home 'Lhasa House' – gathering intelligence on Tibet for the Indian government, and devoting himself to Tibetan scholarship, including the compilation of a Tibetan-English dictionary. Clearly, Sarat Chandra Das was no ordinary pundit, trained only in Montgomerie's ingenious map-making techniques and the use of disguise, but something far closer to the secret service agent Kipling portrays in the character of the Babu.

More, though, lies behind the creation of the talkative Bengali than just his affinities with Chandra Das. Kipling, it is well known, disliked Indian intellectuals, especially Bengali ones, as being too clever by half. Such an attitude was prevalent among Raj officials and other Europeans living in India, who tended to admire those races and tribes with martial qualities. Educated Bengalis were seen as people who questioned the benefits of British rule, and therefore a potential source of trouble. This view was soon to be proved correct, though largely after Kipling had left India. For Bengali nationalists were involved in a campaign of bombings and assassinations during the early 1900s, while in 1915 a German-backed plot to seize control of Calcutta and neighbouring Burma, using armed Bengalis, was uncovered in the nick of time and crushed.

When Kipling was writing *Kim*, he was re-living the happiest period of his life, which had followed a wretchedly unhappy childhood in England away from his parents, so painfully related in his short story 'Baa Baa, Black Sheep'. In contrast, the India he portrays in *Kim* is painted in the rosiest of colours, and much of the book's extraordinary power, which makes us want to rush off to India, is due to this unbridled euphoria. From a safe distance, even Bengali intellectuals had their good points. This explains Kipling's ambivalence towards the Babu. On the one hand he is fat, fawning, garrulous and pompous, ever eager to show off his erudition – almost a caricature of a Bengali intellectual, in fact. On the other he is highly intelligent, moves as 'noise-lessly as a cat', and is brilliant at his job, though he insists that he is 'a fearful man', blaming this on being a Bengali.

Yet before we follow the Babu, Kim and the lama north-wards into the Himalayas, we have one other riddle to solve – one, moreover, that must have puzzled generations of *Kim* readers. It springs from the Babu's disclosure to Kim, shortly before he sets out in pursuit of his quarry, that one of the two Russian intruders is, in fact, a Frenchman. To the Babu this is a welcome piece of news, for he can speak French. But clearly this is not why Kipling brought a Frenchman into the story, for it would have been altogether simpler, not to say more likely, if one of the Russians had spoken English (as it turns out both do). Why then did Kipling make one of his villains a Frenchman, particularly when, for most of his life, he was an ardent Francophile?

Long before, in the early 1800s, there *had* been a French threat to India – even the prospect of a joint invasion by the French and the Russians, with Napoleon marching eastwards across Persia, and the Tsarists thrusting down from the north. But once Napoleon had been forced to abandon his dream of conquering the East, for the best part of a century the Great Game had been waged between Tsarist Russia and Victorian Britain, then the two remaining world super-powers. Indeed, after a brief breathing space, it began again after the Bolshevik Revolution, as Lenin set his sights on India, the richest of all imperial prizes.

In view of this, it seems strange that Kipling should intro-duce a Frenchman into the Great Game without some sort of explanation. There is, however, an explanation, even if he does not provide it, and it is to be found in a now long-forgotten moment in imperial history. In 1891, alarmed by an ambitious and militaristic new Germany, the Russians and the French began to patch up old differences, and two years later signed an alliance which was known to contain secret military agreements. This was reaffirmed in 1899, and a naval convention was subsequently added. In fact it was aimed at Germany, Austria-Hungary and Italy, by whom Paris and St Petersburg felt threatened. But to the British in India, who always feared the worst, it raised once again the Napoleonic spectre of a joint Franco-Russian invasion of the subcontinent. Even apart from this, though, Anglo-French relations were at a low ebb, with the two powers all but going to war in 1898 following a furious incident at Fashoda, on the upper Nile, which both claimed but which Britain acquired. Thus, at the very time when Kipling was planning and writing *Kim*, the British newspapers were filled with rancour and suspicion towards the French, which perhaps explains why he introduced a villainous Frenchman into the plot. But then, in 1904, three years after the book was published, Anglo-French amity was restored with the signing of the Entente Cordiale, which settled all outstanding disagreements (the British tactfully changing the sensitive name of Fashoda to Kodok) and brought Kipling firmly back into the Francophile camp. By then, however, with *Kim* already a best-seller, it was too late for him to change the identity of the villain.

But to return once more to the narrative, now approaching

its denouement. For the next eight pages Kipling treats us to some of the most bewitching descriptive writing in the entire novel, rivalling in its brilliance even his earlier account of Kim's journey with the lama along the Grand Trunk Road. With its sense of freedom, its marvellous freshness, and its distant vistas of great deodar forests and sacred, snow-topped mountains, it brings to the reader a wonderful contentment, and a wish to be walking with them. 'At last they entered a world within a world – a valley of leagues where the high hills were fashioned of the mere rubble and refuse from off the knees of the mountains,' Kipling writes. 'Above them, still enormously above them . . . changeless since the world's beginning, but changing to every mood of sun and cloud, lay out the eternal snow.' Much of its magic, I should add, springs from Kipling's own euphoric memories of escaping from the stifling heat of the plains into the hills around Simla, Mussoorie and Dalhousie during his 'Seven Years' Hard' in Lahore and Allahabad.

Before setting out in pursuit of the Russian and the Frenchman, the Babu had explained his plan to Kim. Posing as sportsmen, the two agents had been secretly stirring up trouble among the northern kings, promising them that very soon a great army would sweep down through the passes and liberate India. Then, to make it seem as though they had never set foot in those parts, and had entered India from the north-east, across the Karakorums, they had marched swiftly eastwards to Leh, the Ladakhi capital. Next, discreetly mapping the route as they travelled, they turned southwards towards the Chini Valley, which lies close to the Tibetan frontier and Mount Kailas, most sacred of all mountains. From there, the Babu believed, they were planning to make their way innocently westwards to Simla, as though they had been shooting in the east all the time, having purchased skins and heads in the market at Leh to remove any possible doubts which might arise. In Simla they intended to dispatch to their shadowy chiefs their secret reports and other dangerously compromising material – using the highly reliable postal service of the unsuspecting Raj authorities. The Babu, who hoped to obtain all their papers on behalf of Colonel Creighton, by fair means or foul, planned to meet up with them somewhere in the Chini Valley and try to worm his way into their confidence.

On leaving Saharunpore, the Babu's anxious final words to Kim had been: 'Please keep your eye on the umbrella . . .' He was referring to the large blue-and-white parasol he carried to shield himself from the searing sun, but also to signal to Kim his whereabouts in the hills and valleys ahead as he marched before them. 'I shall be just four or five miles ahead,' he told Kim.

The route northwards took them first past Dehra Dun, still the headquarters of the Survey of India today, and then, as the real hills began, up past the little hill-station of Mussoorie. I travelled, I must confess, from Saharunpore to Mussoorie by car. Were one to attempt it on foot today one would almost certainly become one of the 200-odd people killed daily on India's roads. Not surprisingly, the authorities are obsessed by road safety, even if few drivers spare it much thought. In addition to the wreckage of cars and lorries,

India's roadsides are garnished with exhortations to still living drivers. 'If you want to give blood,' one I saw read, 'don't give it on the road.' 'Speed', declaimed another, 'has five letters, like Death.' Not all these improving slogans, however, have to do with dangerous driving. 'The largest room in the world', sermonised one, 'is the room for improvement.' Just who composes these homespun homilies, and pays for their display, I failed to discover.

Unlike Kim and the lama, who slept out on the bare hillside, I spent the night in Mussoorie. Set on a horseshoe-shaped ridge, nearly 7,000 feet up in the Himalayan foothills, it is a place – I decided after only twenty minutes – where I would happily spend the rest of my life. To discover why, one should read Ruskin Bond's *Rain in the Mountains*, a beautifully written account of life, past and present, in this little hill-station, by a man who has lived there for over thirty years. It is filled with delightful tales, often comic, of local characters and creatures, especially birds and trees, which are the author's passion, and I defy anyone, after reading it, not to want to sell up and move there immediately. Unfortunately, as it is published in Delhi, it is not easy to obtain in Britain. On the excuse of being a fellow writer, I descended on Ruskin without warning. To my delight I quickly discovered that he too had been brought up on *Kim*, so I was able to discuss with him the route (for Kipling is very vague) that the Babu, Kim and the lama would have taken northwards from Mussoorie into the hills. We finally agreed that Kipling's vagueness was deliberate, and was due to the fact that he had never, on his own admission, 'marched very far' into those misty valleys and hills which lie between Mussoorie and the Chini Valley. There was little point, therefore, in my trying to follow their route on foot – or by pony, as I had intended – as for once Kipling had had to make it up.

I spent my one night in Mussoorie at the once spectacular but now crumbling Savoy Hotel, an ornate monument to

the high days of the Raj, and to the hill-station's own better times. Once, long ago, its corridors had echoed to the foot-steps of the great and the famous, as the early visitors' books show. Queen Mary stayed there, and so did Haile Selassie, Emperor of Ethiopia. That night, however, I appeared to be the only guest in this great mausoleum of a hotel, and I was taken to a once magnificent suite, designed for a rather better class of traveller than myself. Equally empty that night was the cavernous dining-room, which had certainly seen better days. Empty, that is, but for one couple. Exhausted by travelling, I had only dimly noticed them, as they were seated some distance away. Suddenly I heard a cry from their table. 'Peter, what on *earth* are you doing here?' Looking up, I recognised to my amazement two old colleagues from *The Times*. One was David Spanier, once the paper's diplomatic correspondent, and the other his wife, Suzy Menkes, queen of the world's fashion editors, now with the Paris-based *Herald Tribune*. What fates had brought us together in this extremely unlikely spot I cannot imagine, but we shared an evening of newspaper nostalgia. Alas, they were off early next morning, so I saw no more of them.

Even if it now appeared pointless to try to trace the route into the mountains taken by Kim and the lama, at least one could continue to follow their fortunes. As they travelled northwards towards the Chini Valley region, they now and again caught a glimpse of the Babu's blue-and-white parasol far ahead as he struggled slowly up a hillside, or marched along a valley bottom. Day after day, as their journey took them ever higher, the lama noticeably quickened his pace, for the altitude and the cooler air were now getting much closer to those of Tibet. Kim, on the other hand, found the going progressively harder, having spent all his short life on the scorching lowland plains. Never before had he seen such awesome scenery, or so many great mountains. 'Surely the Gods live here!' he gasped breathlessly. 'This is no place for men.'

Today millions of people of differing faiths believe that the Gods do indeed live in these great Himalayan uplands where India and Tibet meet, both spiritually and politically. Here, venerated by Buddhists, Hindus and Jains alike, stands Mount Kailas, 22,000 feet high but forbidden to mountaineers, though many have been tempted. With its beautiful cobalt-blue lake and springs, also sacred, it stands just inside Tibet, where it is regarded as lying at the very centre of the universe. When in 1981 the first Indian pilgrims were allowed there since the Chinese invasion of Tibet, they were dismayed to find that the six monasteries which once stood at the foot of the mountain had been reduced to rubble, some fifteen years earlier, by Red Guards. Similar destruction had also been wrought by the rampaging youths on sacred sites around the hallowed lake. Today, because Peking badly needs the hard currency, foreign tourists can visit Kailas in coach-borne groups.

On the Indian side of the border, closer to where Kim and the lama were travelling, lie two other sacred mountains – Kedarnath and Badrinath – as well as a host of lesser gods' thrones. The taller of these two peaks is Kedarnath, 11,800 feet high, and dedicated to the Hindu deity Shiva, 'the Destroyer'. In times past, scores of Shiva's devotees would fling themselves off the mountainside to their deaths as the ultimate act of worship. The second sacred peak, Badrinath, stands 10,000 feet high, and is dedicated to another Hindu deity, Vishnu, 'the Preserver', who happily makes less dire demands of his devotees. In Kim's day, as they have done for thousands of years, pilgrims trekked through the mountains to worship at these three great giants of nature, though only a handful each year for the journey was arduous and dangerous, and many never returned. Today, every summer, hundreds of thousands of pilgrims, some rich but many in rags, make their way by car, bus, bicycle or on foot to pray for redemption at the many shrines and temples which surround these sacred mountains. As Kim and the lama strode northwards in the Babu's footsteps, they could see both Kedarnath and Badrinath, one behind the other, to their right, though dispiritingly they never seemed to get any further away. Each dawn, wrote Kipling, their twin peaks 'flared windy-red', while during the day 'they lay like molten silver' in the sun's glare.

The Babu had been walking for a week or more (and Kipling is very vague about how long the journey took), when suddenly through his binoculars he spotted two strange white dots on a mountainside some twenty miles ahead. The following day these had moved further down the slope, and the Babu knew instantly that they were tents. Nor, in that remote region, could there be any mistaking whose they were. Struggling through a violent mountain storm, to which, Kipling tells us, 'nine out of ten Englishmen would have given full right of way', and which had Kim and the lama cowering for shelter in a ruined hut, the Babu hastened on. Although soaked to the skin, having come so far he was determined not to let his quarry escape. Eventually, having walked more like forty miles than twenty, because of the many hills he had to circumnavigate, he came upon 'two sodden and rather rheumatic foreigners'.

Ingratiatingly, but with his 'heart beating against his tonsils', he introduced himself to the strangers as 'agent for his

Royal Highness the Raja of Rampur', and asked how he might help them. The two men were clearly relieved to see him, for it transpired that the same thunderstorm which had struck him had also engulfed their camp, the lightning splitting open a pine tree under which they and their bearers were sheltering. At that the men had mutinied, throwing down their loads and vanishing into the surrounding hills, for they had no love for these foreigners who did not behave like proper sahibs and had even threatened them with rifles. The Russian and the Frenchman – for such they clearly were – explained to their new friend that they were anxious to get on to Simla as quickly as possible so that they could get their 'shooting trophies' cured before they began to deteriorate. The Babu, of course, had no doubts about the real reason for their haste. The Post Office, and not the taxidermist, would be their first port of call.

Suddenly, as he was discussing with them what they should do, he spotted one of the deserters skulking among the trees in the distance. After a discreet word with this miscreant, plus a promise of some government silver, the rest of the bearers began sheepishly to reappear. 'My royal master', the Babu told the Russian and the Frenchman, 'will be much annoyed. But these people are onlee common people and grossly ignorant. If your honours will kindly overlook this unfortunate affair, I shall be much pleased.' He very soon learned, however, why it was that the bearers so disliked these sahibs. While pretending to adjust one of their *kiltas* – the large covered baskets which bearers carry on their backs – he happened to knock it over, hoping perhaps to see inside it, only to receive a sharp blow on his wrist by way of admonition. Certainly this did little to endear these two men to him. No English sahib, the Babu told himself, would do such a thing, especially when he had – as they thought – just come to their rescue.

Later that evening the two men pressed strong drink on him, and very soon had him holding forth on the iniquities of British rule. 'He babbled tales of oppression and wrong,' wrote Kipling, 'till the tears ran down his cheeks for the miseries of the land.' Then he staggered off, collapsing beneath a nearby tree to sleep it off. In fact, while lying there snoring, he heard one of the men grumble that they should have sent off their reports from one of the northern kingdoms they had secretly visited, or from Leh, to which his friend replied that the English mails were 'better and safer'. On waking, as though suddenly remembering his treasonable indiscretions, the Babu tried hastily to undo everything that he had said, insisting how much he really loved his British masters, who had bestowed such benefits upon his people. But mockingly the Russian and the Frenchman reminded him of the slanderous words he had used about the British, and gradually he was forced to admit that they were true. When later a delighted Lurgan Sahib heard the full story from the Babu in person, he cursed himself for not having been one of those sodden, sullen bearers who must have listened, quite uncomprehendingly, to this virtuoso lesson in Great Game artifice by such a master of deceit.

Kipling makes no bones about presenting both the Russian, who appears to be in charge of the mission, and the Frenchman in the worst possible light, indeed as little better than stage villains, for he does not even give them names. However, we should not forget that *Kim* was written at a time when British popular feeling – and it was on this that Kipling thrived – was vehemently anti-French, largely because of the ugly incident at Fashoda. It was also highly Russophobic, for a host of reasons, the latest being St Petersburg's attempts to gain a foothold in the Persian Gulf, which the British regarded as India's naval frontier. But Kipling's Francophobia, as we have seen, was comparatively short-lived, so it is his Russophobia, which began in his schooldays in England, which we mainly encounter in his writing. In addition to *Kim*, it surfaces with a vengeance in his chilling short story 'The Man Who Was', written in 1890, and later staged as a play in London, and in his haunting, allegorical poem 'The Truce of the Bear' (1898). Both were written at the height of the Great Game – or the Victorian Cold War as it has sometimes been called – and both, like *Kim*, express Kipling's own intense fear and distrust of the Russians.

In the short story, the officers of Her Majesty's White Hussars at Peshawar are entertaining a young Cossack subaltern named Dirkovich, who has arrived somewhat mysteriously in India from the north, supposedly as the special correspondent of a St Petersburg newspaper. Since their two countries are not actually at war, he is made welcome, and he helps himself liberally to the mess brandy. Suddenly dinner is interrupted by a shot in the darkness outside. A man has been caught trying to crawl past the sentries into the camp.

At first he is assumed to be an Afghan thief, but then it is discovered that he speaks a halting English and that his skin, beneath his filthy rags, is white. His back also bears the terrible scars of the *knout*, the punishment whip used by the Russians. The mysterious stranger is carried, half-conscious, into the mess, where he breaks down and begins to weep, bitterly and inconsolably as a child, before the silent throng of officers. Given a glass of brandy, he begins to revive a little and look around him. Then, to everyone's astonishment, he shows signs of recognising some of the mess trophies and paintings.

Suddenly the Cossack guest, who has slumped drunkenly to the floor, rises to his feet. Catching sight of his uniform, the stranger becomes hysterical and grovels at his feet. 'Dirkovich', wrote Kipling, 'made no offer to raise him', though one of the British officers gently helps him to his feet. The dreadful truth now begins to emerge. It transpires from the regimental records, which someone has gone to find, that some thirty years earlier a subaltern from the White Hussars had been reported missing, later presumed dead, during the Crimean War. It turns out that this half-crazed individual is that officer. After his capture he was incarcerated in Siberia for insulting a Tsarist officer. Much later he managed to escape, living for years in the forest before finally reaching India, and finding his way back to his old regiment – only just in time, for three days later he dies, to be buried with full military honours, back at last in the bosom of his regiment. Dirkovich, needless to say, is politely hurried on his way, hinting darkly that one day he will return with an invading army through the Khyber Pass. Curiously, the dramatised West End stage version of this story was first performed in 1907, the very year which brought the Great Game to an end, with the signing of the Anglo-Russian Convention.

But the Victorian Cold War with Russia still had nine years to run when Kipling wrote his poem – or rather polemic – 'The Truce of the Bear'. In it he tells the gruesome tale, which the Raj historian General MacMunn insists is true, of the blind old beggar Matun. Fifty years earlier, then a smallholder, he had set off in pursuit of a bear which had been destroying his crops and killing his goats. Finally he comes face to face with it, and raises his matchlock to shoot it. But suddenly it rises to its feet like a man, its paws 'like hands in prayer', begging to be spared. Touched with pity for this strange, half-human creature, Matun momentarily lowers his weapon. In a split second the bear has struck, tearing off Matun's entire face with its cruel, razor-sharp claws and leaving him hideously deformed – 'eyeless, noseless and lipless', and hardly able to speak. Every summer, though, he tries to warn sahibs shooting in this region of the terrible danger of trusting 'the Bear that walks like a man', raising the bandage which covers what little remains of his face to convince them. General MacMunn, writing in 1937 after a lifetime spent in India, says that while he never encountered the bear – Adam-zad it is called, meaning 'born of Adam' – he did encounter one of its luckless victims near Simla.

'I heard a whimper,' he recounts, 'a half-strangled call for pity. I looked towards the sound and saw, leaning on a staff, a man, or at least I thought it was a man.' It was, he went on, 'a head without a face ... no nose, no eyes, hardly even an eye-socket, and a hole like a rotten medlar where the mouth should have been'. As the poor creature whimpered again, his groom, a hillman, told him: 'A bear has done that, sahib – an old black bear; torn his face off with his claws.' And that, Kipling's grim poem warns us, is precisely what the Russians will do to you if you are foolish enough to trust them, or lower your guard for a second.

I must confess, having devoted much time to examining the record of the Tsarists during the Great Game years, with their repeated broken promises, that I am forced to share Kipling's view of Russian duplicity. And everything that has happened since – during both world wars, between the wars, and throughout the long years of the Cold War – has simply reinforced that view. Even since the death of Communism, which appeared to promise a fresh start, it transpires that the Russians, in breach of solemnly signed agreements, have continued to manufacture chemical and biological weapons, and to spy on the West. As Kipling put it in the final line of his poem: *'There is no truce with Adam-zad, the Bear that looks like a man!'*

But one last question still remains to be answered. On which, if any, real-life travellers or individuals did Kipling model his two villainous pseudo-sportsmen? Momentarily leaving the Babu – by now anxiously casting around for Kim and the lama – with the two intruders as they head for Simla, we will look briefly at the two most likely candidates.

Both, to the dismay of the Raj authorities, had been discovered in 1887 on the Indian side of the frontier after crossing undetected over the northern passes from Tsarist Central Asia.

# 14

# *The River of the Arrow*

IN THE SUMMER of that year, alarming reports reached Simla that three Russian explorers had secretly entered India from the north. After crossing the Pamirs, then still deep in snow, and the strategically sensitive Baroghil Pass, they had turned up in the northern kingdom of Chitral. There they were detained by the ruler who immediately sought instructions from the Indian government – from whom he received an annual subsidy – on what to do with these trespassers. Eventually they were brought under armed escort to Simla, where they were interviewed in person by Lord Dufferin, the Viceroy.

It soon transpired, to everyone's relief, that they were not Russians after all, but French, led by the well-known explorer Gabriel Bonvalot. Although Bonvalot himself was a frank admirer of the Russians, the French were not then regarded in India as a threat, for this was some years before the Franco-

Russian alliance or the Fashoda affair. Only later, when Bon-valot's book appeared, did it emerge that he and his compatriots had been actively encouraged by a Russian general in Samarkand to try to cross the Pamirs into northern India – no doubt to see how easily this might be accomplished.

Bonvalot's description of their nightmarish ride over the Pamirs came as a considerable relief to India's defence chiefs. For though the Frenchmen had chosen the best time of year to make their crossing – a time when the passes were considered most vulnerable to hostile penetration – these highly experienced travellers had very nearly perished, losing their horses and baggage, and reaching Chitral virtually destitute. If they, travelling fast and unencumbered, had run into such difficulties, then an invading army, dragging guns and other heavy equipment across the passes, might expect to face almost insuperable problems.

But despite the political sensitivity of their crossing from Tsarist Central Asia into India, it had nonetheless been a remarkable and courageous achievement. Once their identities had been established, therefore, they were made welcome in Simla, where Lockwood Kipling, who was on close terms with the Viceroy, helped to entertain them. Rudyard was then working in Allahabad, and almost certainly never met them, but he would undoubtedly have heard the full story from his father. As a reporter on the *Pioneer*, moreover, he would have known, from the paper's correspondent in Simla, of the consternation that their arrival had caused there. In view of all this, it seems more than likely that the pro-Russian

Bonvalot was the inspiration for the fictional Frenchman in *Kim*. For reasons of libel, however, if not of common decency, Kipling could not draw too close a likeness between the real-life French explorer, who was still very much alive when *Kim* was published in 1901, and the fictional one, whom he depicts as a blackguard. There is only one other possible candidate from whom Kipling might have borrowed, and that is a French carpet expert called Dauvergne, who was helping the Kashmiris to develop their textile industry. A keen traveller, he accompanied both British and Russian parties in this region, though usually he journeyed alone. However, he appears to have been as pro-British as pro-Russian, for he helped to erect the lonely monument on the Karakorum Pass to the murdered Scottish Great Game player Andrew Dalgleish.

There is an additional reason for associating Bonvalot, in Kipling's mind, with his fictional Frenchman. In Bonvalot's subsequent account of their Pamir crossing, he tells of their meeting with a certain Captain Gromchevsky – 'a very hardy young officer' – who had travelled widely in the Pamirs and who gave them valuable advice about routes and conditions there. This is the formidable Gromchevsky who, less than a year later, was to cause near panic in Simla by entering Hunza, in Russian uniform and with a small escort of Cossacks, where he was reported to have been well received by the ruler, and to have promised to return the following year with some interesting, if unspecified, proposals from the Tsar. This led to the hasty dispatch to Hunza of Captain Francis Younghusband, then an up-and-coming star in the Great

Game, with instructions to find out precisely what was going on. I have told the story of their encounter in *The Great Game*, so will not repeat it here. But it seems almost certain that the Russian in *Kim* was inspired by Gromchevsky for there was really no other candidate around at that time, or even subsequently. Kipling would certainly have known all about Gromchevsky, since his penetration of Hunza caused even more of a sensation in British India than had the arrival of Bonvalot in Chitral. The fact that Gromchevsky and Bonvalot knew one another, and were both bent on crossing into India, is perhaps not without significance.

\*

When we left the Babu, he and his Russian and French friends were hurrying westwards from the Chini Valley towards Simla, which the two foreigners were anxious to reach as soon as possible. The road they took – the old Tibetan trade route – was narrow and winding in those days, not to say slow-going, as Kipling himself had discovered. In the spring of 1885, while recovering from dysentery, he set out eastwards along it from Simla with two friends. On the first day they only managed to cover eight miles in five hours of walking. After a day's rest, admiring the ravishing mountain scenery, they set out again, this time covering eleven miles. 'Legs', noted Kipling in his diary, 'getting used to ground.' But he never got much further than the village of Kotgarh, renowned for its apples, some fifty miles from Simla, and that took him nearly six days, plus a further five getting back to Simla.

However, the experience was far from wasted on Kipling. On his last day he encountered a violent thunderstorm, 'which exploded in our midst' – clearly the model for the one that the Babu and the others ran into. 'We were all flung on our faces,' wrote Kipling in *Something of Myself*. Seconds later he saw a bolt of lightning split a fully grown pine tree from top to bottom, and send it spinning away down the mountainside. In *Kim* the sight of this was enough to make the Russian and the Frenchman's bearers drop their loads and flee, but Kipling's own men remained steadfastly at his side.

The Babu, who had to travel three times as far along this track as had Kipling, was meanwhile keeping an anxious look-out for Kim and the lama, who by that time should have been somewhere very close. It was with some relief, therefore, that he came upon them by the roadside. The lama was sitting cross-legged above a curious-looking chart, held down with stones, the mysteries of which he was busily explaining to Kim. Kim, in fact, had spotted the Babu's striped parasol some way off, and had suggested to the lama that they wait there for him. The lama, of course, still believed the Bengali to be an itinerant doctor travelling into these out-of-the-way parts to treat patients.

One of the foreigners asked what the old man was doing. 'He is expounding holy picture,' the Babu explained. Then, while the two looked on, the Babu quickly whispered to Kim that all their secret reports, maps and letters – including a very damning one from a northern king – were in the large *kilta* with the red cover. 'They guard it most carefully,' he hissed, remembering the blow he had received when he knocked it over. Then one of the men – the Russian – asked whether the lama would sell him his holy picture. The old man refused. 'All Tibet is full of cheap reproductions of the Wheel,' wrote Kipling, 'but the lama was an artist, as well as a wealthy abbot.' The Russian, angered by this unclean Tibetan who dared to haggle with him over a grubby bit of paper, held out a handful of rupees and snatched at the flimsy chart, which promptly tore in half. Instinctively and angrily, the old man reached for his heavy iron pen-case – 'the priest's weapon', he called it – for he had spent many days drawing this Wheel of Life for his beloved *chela*. But the Russian was too quick for him, and before Kim could stop him, he had struck the lama full in the face.

At that, all hell broke loose on the mountainside. Kim, his Irish blood at boiling-point, hurled himself furiously on the Russian, seizing him by the throat, and the next moment, fighting viciously, the two were tumbling down the steep slope together. Shocked by the two appalling acts of sacrilege they had witnessed – the tearing of the sacred chart, and the violence towards the lama – the bearers now turned and fled with their loads. 'They have taken the baggage and all the guns,' screamed the Frenchman to his colleague, discharging his revolver blindly after them. Then, intending to take the old man hostage, he ran towards where he sat, dazed and bruised. But he was met by a hail of sharp stones from the bearers, who had guessed his intention, and one of them darted back and seized the lama, sweeping him off up the mountainside to join the others.

Here the quick-thinking Babu saw his chance of getting his hands on the *kilta* with the red cover. Running over to where Kim was grimly banging the Russian's head against a rock, he pretended to rescue the man by dragging his young assailant off him. At the same time he whispered to Kim to follow the bearers and not let the red-covered *kilta* out of his sight. As Kim raced up the hill, a bullet fired by the Frenchman narrowly missed him. The Babu yelled to him

to stop shooting lest the angry bearers return and murder them all. Indeed, the bearers were all for killing the foreigners with their own rifles to appease the wrath of the gods. 'He struck the Holy One – we saw it!' cried one of them. 'Our cattle will be barren – our wives will cease to bear. The snows will slide upon us as we go home.' But the lama, mastering his own wrath, albeit with much difficulty, ordered that there must be no killing, no acts of revenge. 'They will be born many times – in torment,' he assured the bearers, before collapsing exhausted at Kim's feet.

That, in essence, is what happened when the dark forces of the material world, represented by the Russian and the Frenchman, were made by Kipling to collide with those of the spirit, embodied in the saintly Tibetan. In this sudden and violent episode, the dramatic highlight of the book, Kipling's Russophobia, not to mention his Francophobia, is undisguised and quite unashamed. Neither of the two foreigners is allowed a single redeeming quality. Certainly in their rough treatment of the Babu, as well as the coolies, Kipling compares them unfavourably with the British, using their men's words to condemn them. 'They are not true sahibs,' says one contemptuously. In those more gentlemanly times, it was highly unusual for a serious writer – in 1907 he was to win the Nobel Prize for Literature – to portray national types as such out-and-out villains. But Kipling's feelings could run very high, and he was safe in the knowledge that most of his readers at that time regarded both the Russians and the French, especially in combination, as a deadly threat to Britain's imperial paramountcy.

Kipling, a man of action frustrated by defective eyesight, clearly relishes describing the men's humiliating downfall at the hands of the Babu and Kim, not to mention the angry bearers. This is particularly manifest in a book otherwise so tranquil. But this tranquillity soon returns, as Kim and the bearers, greatly fearing for the lama's life, fall over one another in their efforts to attend to him. 'Have they hurt him to the death?' asked one, as Kim knelt anxiously over the old man, listening to his heart. Then one of the men produced a bottle of cheap whisky – 'the medicine of sahibs', he called it – apparently looted from one of the *kiltas*, and forced some between the unconscious lama's lips. More followed, and the old man's heart began to respond. For good measure, a little was also rubbed on his chest, and before long he sat up, coughing and groping for his prayer-beads. Though weak and bruised, he appeared none the worse for wear. So they decided to rest where they were until the moon rose, and then by its light to trek to the tiny village of Shamlegh-under-the-Snow, some hours away, where no pursuers would expect to find them. There they would share the contents of the *kiltas* between them, throw the rest down the mountainside, and then go swiftly on their way, remembering, they agreed, 'that we have never seen or taken service with these sahibs'.

While the men rested and the lama slept, Kim considered the day's extraordinary adventures. Here, rendered harmless, 'were the emissaries of the dread Power of the North, very possibly as great in their own land as Mahbub or Colonel Creighton'. And it was he and the Babu who, with a certain amount of luck, had brought this about. The Russian, he guessed, would be lame for a while, for he had kicked the man viciously in the groin during their fight. His one regret, however, was that he had not shot him dead with Mahbub Ali's revolver for striking the Holy One. He comforted himself with the thought that these men who had tried to suborn the northern kings now slept on the bare mountainside, robbed of everything, including their rifles and secret papers. Indeed, at that very moment, half-frozen and hungry, they were desperately trying to decide what to do, turning ill-temperedly to the Babu for advice. Appearing to show great concern for their safety, he warned them to steer well clear of the Raja of Rampur, his own master, who would certainly imprison them if he discovered that they had struck a holy man. Their best plan of action, he suggested, would be to reach the safety of Simla as quickly as possible, where they would no longer be in danger of arrest – or attack by their angry former bearers, now armed with rifles.

When, shortly before dawn, Kim and the others reached Shamlegh-under-the-Snow, they found a tiny hamlet of three or four mud-and-timber huts occupied by graziers, who lived there only during the summer months. That no such place as Shamlegh ever existed, save in Kipling's imagination, I am fairly sure, for although names change over the years, I have combed numerous large-scale Survey of India maps of his day without finding any trace of it. Kipling, moreover, never got any further than Kotgarh, and Shamlegh-under-the-Snow, if it ever existed, would lie a hundred miles or more further east. Thus Kipling appears to have made it up, which is further borne out by old Simla hands I consulted who told me they had never heard of this place. It is remotely possible, of course, that Kipling heard of it from someone else who had actually been there, for it is vividly described. Anyone determined to try and find it can now drive most of the way there from Simla along a tortuous mountain road which will take them to the Chini Valley, now renamed the Sangla Valley, or Baspa Valley. From there they are on their own, and with *Kim* in hand will have to proceed on foot for several hours, though in what direction I must leave them to decide. By luck, though, they might find a local guide who knows a man whose uncle thinks he knows where it is.

If Shamlegh-under-the-Snow does, or once did, exist, there is one striking clue to its whereabouts. Immediately behind it, Kipling tells us, there is a sheer drop of some two thousand feet into an abyss as dark as 'interstellar space', and where 'never yet man has set foot'. It is on the very brink of this great pit, which Kipling calls Shamlegh-midden, that the frail huts teeter, the three families occupying them tossing their refuse straight out of the window and out of sight far below. If, armed with these few clues, and reinforced perhaps by locally acquired knowledge, anyone does find Shamlegh-under-the-Snow, I would be only too grateful to hear from them.

It was into this grim refuse dump that the gleeful bearers, having shared out the contents of the *kiltas*, finally tossed all that was left, aware that no one would ever think of searching down there for evidence of their crime. By allowing the handful of graziers a share too (their womenfolk got the aluminium pots, as well as the tents from which to make clothes), they had made them accessories and thus bought their silence. Kim's prize, of course, was the red-topped *kilta*, filled with the expedition's secrets, things that the others neither wanted nor understood. After the bearers had left in triumph – four of them brandishing expensive new sporting rifles – Kim settled down in the privacy of one of the huts to explore his own haul.

There were maps, diaries, letters, books and valuable survey instruments. But it was not until Kim got to the very bottom of the *kilta* that he found what he most wanted – 'a sealed, gilded and illuminated document such as one king sends to another'. Since they had a long way to travel, Kim now had to decide what to keep and what to reject, for the *kilta* was far too heavy for him to carry while at the same time supporting the frail lama. He carefully put aside all the letters, maps and diaries – which the Russian had been heard to say represented their eight months' work among the northern kings – and for which he knew Colonel Creighton would give his eye-teeth. Rejecting the heavy compasses, theodolites and other map-making instruments, he stuffed them back into the *kilta*, which he then tossed through the hut window into the abyss below. 'The wheeling basket', wrote Kipling, 'vomited its contents as it dropped. The theodolite hit a jutting cliff ledge and exploded like a shell.' Peering down into the void, Kim strained his ears for the noise of the impact as it struck the bottom, but no sound came up from below.

# The River of the Arrow

It was after the bearers had gone that Kim met the Woman of Shamlegh, a rather tragic figure on whom I shall not dwell overlong here as she has little or nothing to do with the Great Game aspects of *Kim*. This woman, whom we first encounter in Kipling's short story 'Lispeth', written in 1886, has suffered a disastrous love affair with an English traveller, whom she has nursed back to health at the Christian mission at Kotgarh, and is determined to marry. He promises to return, but never does. Disillusioned by Christianity, she goes back to her own hill-folk, trying to forget. But years later, on meeting Kim, she is suddenly and bitterly reminded of the sahib she once loved. She makes pathetic overtures to him, only to be rejected once again. Some politically correct critics have suggested that Kim only spurns her because she is an Indian and he a European. But this is laughable. For a start she must be old enough to be his own mother (in 'Lispeth', written five years earlier, Kipling describes her as 'wrinkled'). Secondly, as we know, Kim has very urgent Great Game matters on his hands – not to mention the fact that he is supposed to be the celibate *chela* of a Buddhist holy man. However, he does use her to carry a secret message to the Babu, who has not yet set out for Simla, to say that he has secured all the secret papers, and is about to head for the Sahiba's farmhouse at Saharunpore with the lama.

Despite Kim's rebuff, though, the kind-hearted Woman of Shamlegh insisted on giving him money for the journey, and provided five men – for she was the power in that tiny community – to carry the lama down to the plains in a *dooli*, the simple litter of the hills. Two of these men, whom she appeared to regard with disdain, were her own husbands for, through economic necessity, theirs was a polyandrous society. Grateful to her for her kindness, Kim put his arm around her waist and kissed her on the cheek. Then, rather awkwardly, they shook hands. 'Goodbye,' she said, adding wistfully: 'You will come back again?' Half an hour later, wrote Kipling, Kim looked back, and glimpsed 'a tiny figure at the hut door waving a white rag'. At which the lama observed quietly: 'She has acquired merit beyond all others.'

\*

Leaving Kim and his little caravan heading slowly down to Saharunpore, for their route is far too vaguely described to try to follow, I went instead by road, stopping off in Dehra Dun on the way. I had always wanted to see the original headquarters of the Great Trigonometrical Survey of India – to give it its full title. It was from here, in the 1860s, that Colonel Montgomerie trained his hand-picked native explorers in ingenious secret surveying techniques, and then unleashed them into forbidden and hitherto unmapped parts of Central Asia. Here, too, were his workshops where compasses, notebooks and thermometers were cunningly concealed in Buddhist prayer-wheels and pilgrims' staves. And here also he and his colleagues translated the material they brought back into maps of the little-known regions beyond India's northern frontiers.

I very soon realised, though, that by my own efforts alone I stood no chance of penetrating the great campus-like complex which today houses the Survey's many departments and buildings. For much of its work is highly sensitive, with obvious military implications, thus making it a target for terrorists and others. Understandably, therefore, in a country virtually at war with its neighbour, inquisitive foreigners like myself can hardly expect just to stroll in off the street and be shown around. Not fully realising this, and having only allowed myself one day in Dehra Dun, the chances of seeing the pundits' old haunts now appeared pretty remote.

But then I had a sudden stroke of luck of the kind that can only happen in India. Anxious to obtain a copy of Ruskin Bond's account of life in Mussoorie, I wandered into The Green Bookshop, which was just down the road from my hotel. On the owner's desk, by an extraordinary chance, was a pile of my own books, about to be sent off, it turned out, to a school in Mussoorie. Somewhat sheepishly, I introduced myself to Mr Upendra Arora, the distinguished-looking proprietor, explaining what had brought me to Dehra Dun. Now booksellers in India enjoy a somewhat privileged position. For among the educated élite, almost everybody who is anybody passes through their shops, often stopping for a long chat about some intellectual or literary issue. As a result, they know just about everyone of consequence. Mr Arora proved to be no exception, immediately springing into action on my behalf, speaking by telephone to someone – one of his regular customers, no doubt – highly placed in the Survey hierarchy. Then, putting down the phone, he got out his car and drove me across town to the complex which now houses the Survey, and where still stands the headquarters of Montgomerie's day.

That, admittedly, was only the beginning, for there followed much waiting around, letter-writing – including one to the Surveyor-General himself – and form-filling. But at least, thanks to Mr Arora, I was inside. Finally, I was escorted across the lawns to the original Survey building, which dates from 1823. Fittingly it has been converted into a small private museum commemorating the Survey's work over the past two and a quarter centuries. A handsome, yellow-washed building with a clock-tower, it contains bronze statues of its founding fathers, including Sir George Everest, after whom the mountain is controversially named, faded portraits of other famous surveyors, examples of early instruments, and displays showing the work of the Survey today. But what really gladdened my heart were the busts of Nain Singh, Kishen Singh and Kintup, three of the greatest of the pundits. Also displayed was Montgomerie's own box of surveying instruments. I confess to a strong feeling of awe as I stood in that marble-floored room beneath the gyrating ceiling fans, knowing that it was here that Montgomerie gave his final instructions to these remarkable men whom he knew he might well be sending to their deaths. I could imagine his joy, moreover, on hearing that a pundit, from whom no word had been received for many months, even years, was on his way home, and would shortly be standing on the very same spot that I was.

*

For Kim and the lama, in contrast to their idyllic and carefree trek northwards to the Chini Valley, the return journey proved to be a nightmarish one, especially for Kim. So long as they enjoyed the services of the Shamlegh men and their *dooli*, in which the lama, still bruised and shaken, rode, they were able to travel some twelve miles a day. But when they got down to the plains, and it was time for the men to return home, this was reduced to no more than two. For not only did Kim have to support the old man's weight as they walked, but he also bore the burden of the captured maps and papers, not to mention their blankets and other essentials. And whenever they halted in some small hamlet, instead of resting, Kim had to beg for food and see to the lama's needs. Very soon the physical strain began to tell on him, and he realised that he was sickening for something. Finally, when they were still about twenty miles short of Saharunpore, and had travelled less than a mile that day, he knew he could go no further. He managed, however, to get a villager to go to the Sahiba's farmhouse and beg her to send a litter for the lama. Then, overcome by exhaustion and worry, he broke down in tears at the old man's feet. The Sahiba, fortunately, acted swiftly, and soon the lama – filled with remorse at overtaxing his young *chela*'s strength – was being borne in her personal palanquin. When they reached the farm, the Sahiba realised that Kim was ill and immediately took charge of him, making him sleep for many hours, giving him strengthening dishes and prescribing him strange potions that restore a man's well-being.

My own journey by car to Saharunpore was shamefully comfortable, taking me through the heart of the beautiful, forested Siwalik Hills, with monkeys once again lining the roadside in their hundreds, and finally down into the great mango orchards which surround the town. Instinctively I found myself looking out for the Sahiba's 'long white rambling house', and for an instant I thought I had spotted it – a long, low, whitewashed farmhouse, set in an orchard, some five or six miles out of Saharunpore. Fleetingly, I considered driving up to the farm and asking the owner if he or she had ever read *Kim*, and if so whether Kipling could possibly have had their farmhouse in mind when he described the Sahiba's. But, fortunately perhaps, my driver had carried me some distance past the gateway by the time I had thought about it, and by then it was too late to turn back.

In fact, I was not the first person to try to pinpoint the Sahiba's farmhouse, even if mine was not exactly a serious attempt. I recall reading in the journal of the Kipling Society some time ago an account by an Australian member, then living in India, who had spent several days, *Kim* in hand, trying to locate its whereabouts. Armed with a map, and working on the assumption that Kipling had a real farmhouse in mind, he entered into discussions with local land registry officials and others, though in the end he had to admit defeat. Nonetheless, drawing on clues scattered through *Kim*, and with the aid of co-ordinates based on these, he worked out on the map where he reckoned it should have been. Strangely enough, a year or two back, a real farmhouse in this somewhat obscure town suddenly found itself on the front pages of the world's newspapers. Three young Britons, kidnapped in Delhi by a Muslim terrorist group, were held hostage there in chains until freed by Indian special forces who stormed their prison.

# The River of the Arrow

While Kim was slowly recovering under the skilled minis-
trations of the Sahiba, the Babu was hastening down to
Saharunpore to relieve him of the maps and letters. He had
left the unhappy Russian and Frenchman at the doors of the
Alliance Bank on the Simla Mall, where they hoped to obtain
some kind of assistance. On parting, they had given him a
letter commending him for his valuable services to them.
Such a letter, he pointed out, might prove very useful were
other 'friends' to come over the passes from the north. For
he had left them with the impression that he, together with
'millions of fellow-serfs', looked forward eagerly to the day
when the Tsar would deliver them from the British.

Anxious lest something untoward should happen to the
captured papers before they could be seen by Colonel Creighton and others in Simla, the Babu – 'once fat . . . now lean
and weather-worn' – headed for Saharunpore with surprising
speed, hoping to catch up with the slow-moving Kim and
the lama. On reaching the farmhouse not far behind them, he
was dismayed to learn of Kim's illness. Worse, the formidable
Sahiba refused to allow anyone to enter his sickroom. In
fact, the crucial maps and letters, which Kim had told her
were sacred texts, were locked safely away in a box beside
the bed. Unaware of this, however, the Babu was left to fret
for an entire week until Kim was well enough, in the Sahiba's
view, to see him. Indeed, so anxious was he about the whereabouts of the papers that he sent a message to Mahbub Ali
to seek his help.

When, finally, the Sahiba deemed the patient sufficiently
recovered to see the Babu, he hastened in, closing the door

behind him. To his immense relief Kim pointed to the box, handing him the key. 'All that was handwritten in the *kilta* I took,' he told the Babu, who began excitedly to examine some of the letters. Reading aloud from one of these, written by one of the northern kings, the Babu declared with glee: 'He will have to explain offeecially how the deuce-an'-all he is writing love letters to the Tsar.' Three or four prime ministers, he added, also appeared to be implicated in the correspondence. The repercussions from this treasonable affair, he told Kim, would be profound. To Kim's immense relief he officially took possession of all the papers and maps whose weight, and worry, had greatly contributed to his collapse. He was, after all, still only a schoolboy in years, and to some Kipling scholars his breakdown was, to quote one, 'physical, psychological, emotional, moral, all rolled into one'. If so, it must be said, he managed to get over it remarkably quickly.

Kim's principal concern, however, on coming round, was not the secret papers, which the Babu was about to take in triumph to Simla, but the lama, whose welfare he had been unable to attend to during his illness. 'Where is my Holy One?' he demanded of one of the Sahiba's servants. It was then that he discovered that something of momentous importance had taken place while he was recovering. The lama had found his sacred river. The Search was over.

It had happened in a most extraordinary and unexpected way. While Kim was on his sick-bed, the lama had found himself facing a crisis of his own. Filled with self-reproach at his own actions, he had slipped away from the farmhouse, and spent two days and nights beneath a tree, fasting and meditating. For not only had he allowed himself to be lured away from the Search by the prospect of returning to his beloved hills, when he knew in his heart that enlightenment did not lie there, but he had also given way to the Red Mist of Anger when struck by the Russian, and now had brought about the illness of his devoted *chela*. Suddenly, on his second night of meditation, he beheld the truth of all things. 'My Soul went free,' he explained to an uncomprehending Kim later. It had, he added, 'passed beyond the illusion of Time and Space and of Things'.

At this divine moment the Babu, who had come looking for him in case he knew of the captured papers' whereabouts, chose to shake him by the shoulder. For a second he feared that the old man was suffering a cataleptic or epileptic fit, or was even dying. From afar off, the lama heard the Babu's voice asking: 'What shall come to the boy if thou art dead?' Overcome with love and compassion for his *chela*, who had assisted him so dutifully in his quest, the lama tore himself away from the 'Great Soul', that final extinction of the self, determined to win salvation for Kim too. Staggering to his feet, and shaking off the Babu's restraining hand, he heard a voice cry: 'The River! Take heed for the River!' Believing the voice to be divine and informing him that the River of the Arrow lay at his feet, he plunged into the water of the irrigation channel which flowed a few feet away from where he had been meditating, thereby cleansing both himself and Kim from all worldly sin. Leaping in after him lest he drown, the Babu pulled him out and, with the help of Mahbub Ali, who had just arrived, carried him back to the farmhouse, where the Sahiba roundly scolded him for adding to her worries.

It may seem bizarre to the reader that the lama's River of the Arrow turned out to be an irrigation channel on the Sahiba's mango farm. But what the Tibetan was really seeking during the Search – those three years of wandering the length and breadth of India – was enlightenment. This, Kipling appears to be saying, comes only from knowledge gained through meditation, and could happen anywhere. The washing away of sins was purely symbolic. At that point, any river would have done.

It is during the closing pages of *Kim* that there arises a question which Kipling leaves unanswered, and which critics have ever since tried to resolve. Throughout the narrative, the teenage Kim has moved easily between two ultimately irreconcilable worlds – the saintly world of the lama, and the cruel, material one of the Great Game. Now that he is about to enter adulthood, he must choose between them. Mahbub Ali, who first spotted this prodigy for his Great Game masters, is concerned lest Kim choose to remain with his Holy One, the attractions of whose way of life the worldly Afghan fails to understand.

The book ends with Kim and the lama sitting peacefully together among the mango groves surrounding the Sahiba's house, just as night is beginning to fall. The old Tibetan, who we know has not long to live, has just described to Kim how his long Search has ended. In Kipling's original manuscript, now in the British Library, he closes the story with the beautiful words: 'He crossed his hands on his lap, as a man may who has gone through the Valley of the Shadow and knows what is beyond.' But then he had second thoughts, for he changed the end of that sentence to: '. . . as a man may who has won salvation for himself and his beloved.' He did this presumably so as to include Kim in the book's concluding sentence, thus rounding off his narrative. That still leaves unresolved the question of where Kim's heart and future really lay – whether he would choose to follow the lama, perhaps back into Tibet, or enter the harsh world of Mahbub Ali. It can be argued either way, and frequently is, but only Kipling knew the answer. And that is another story – one which he never wrote.

My own quest now over, I had no further excuse for lingering among the ghosts of Kipling's Great Game. I drove straight from Saharunpore to Delhi airport and caught the next plane home.

# 'When everyone is dead . . .'

I F, FOR REASONS of his own, Kipling chose not to tell us what became of Kim (although his correspondence suggests that in 1902 he did briefly toy with a sequel), in 1987 an Indian novelist, T. N. Murari, had no such qualms when he wrote *The Imperial Agent: The Sequel to Kipling's Kim*. This Murari rounded off the following year with *The Last Victory*, a sequel to that sequel, taking Kim through the First World War and ending with his death, in dramatic circumstances, in 1919. Both books, now not easy to find, are cleverly written and skilfully plotted, though they fall well short of Kipling's masterpiece. Moreover, given the strange things that happen in India, Murari's narrative is far from improbable. Anyone intending to read these two books would be advised to skip my next two paragraphs, for I am going to reveal what, in Murari's view, became of Kim – not to mention Colonel Creighton, who appears in both books.

For a start we discover that Kim has chosen the twilight world of Colonel Creighton and Mahbub Ali in preference to that of the lama – a choice that clearly offers Murari far greater narrative scope. There is no touching final farewell to the old man, Murari leaving that unsaid, although Kim's character has clearly deepened as a result of the saintly Tibetan's influence. Instead, Kim finds himself investigating a plot, by Indian revolutionaries, to assassinate Lord Curzon by steering the viceregal train over a mountainside on its way down from Simla. Despite Kim's protests, a totally innocent Indian is arrested and sentenced to twenty-four years' imprisonment for attempted murder and sedition. Gradually Kim comes to see British rule in India as repressive, with even Creighton prepared to use unscrupulous means to gain greater powers for the security services. Before long Kim himself becomes a victim of those powers. Wrongfully arrested as a revolutionary, he is beaten and imprisoned with other convicted troublemakers. When Creighton learns of this, he is dismayed, but asks Kim to remain in jail so that he may win the confidence of the other prisoners and thus penetrate their organisation and learn their secrets. Instead, Kim finds himself increasingly in sympathy with the revolutionaries, and he refuses to co-operate with Creighton.

Murari's first book ends with Kim deciding that from now on, despite being born a sahib, his allegiance lies with the Indians, and that in future he will be playing against Creighton, whom he once loved like a father, in the Great Game for India's destiny. Murari's second book, embracing the years 1913 to 1919, opens with Creighton receiving a knight-hood for his success in outmanoeuvring the Raj's foes (inci-dentally Murari erroneously calls him Sir John Creighton, though in *Kim* he is William). We also see Kim marrying an Indian revolutionary, who bears him a daughter. After an unsuccessful attempt by Creighton to have him eliminated, Kim is finally shot down by British troops at Amritsar in April 1919 – the notorious, real-life massacre in which, on General Dyer's orders, 380 angry but unarmed demonstrators were killed, and many more injured. Lastly, in revenge for Kim's death, his young widow kills Colonel Creighton, by then retired, with a revolver. Yet, although Murari tells his dramatic tale extremely well, his two books are today little known, while *Kim* – Kipling's supreme achievement, by which he will always be remembered – goes on for ever, with new edition after new edition, and another film version, the third, on the way.

But if *Kim* goes on down the generations, so too does the Great Game, even to this day. Kipling himself forecast this in 1901, six years before the Anglo-Russian Convention – which apportioned spheres of interest between London and St Petersburg – seemingly brought it all to an end. 'When everyone is dead the Great Game is finished. Not before,' declared the Babu to Kim. 'The Great Game that never ceases day and night,' mused Lurgan Sahib. With the signing of the convention, it did in fact cease, though only tempor-arily. For during the First World War, when Britain and Russia were allies, the Germans and the Turks – with their covetous eyes on India and Tsarist Central Asia – together opened a brief new chapter in the Great Game. Seeking to destabilise them, and thereby make them ripe for plucking, they sent secret missions into these regions under the banner of a holy war. But their defeat in 1918 once more brought this shadowy game to an end – though not for very long. Immediately after the Russian Revolution, Lenin began to show imperialist ambitions of his own towards British India, declaring that he intended to liberate it, and the rest of the East, with the heady new gospel of Marxism.

This task Stalin readily took over on his accession, although he had singularly little success. Finally, in June 1941, the Nazi invasion of Russia forced him into the war on the Allied side, thereby ending any ambitions he might have had of absorbing India into the Bolshevik empire. Six years later the British packed their bags and left India for good, bringing the long Anglo-Russian chapter of the Great Game to an end after more than a century. But even that, as Kipling had foretold in the words of the Babu, was not the end of the Great Game. For today 'the new Great Game', as the political analysts and head-line-writers have christened it, is being played from one end of the map of Asia to the other. Colonel Creighton, peering down from the Valhalla of the Great Game, would have no difficulty in recognising today's rivalries in the region as merely a continuation of the old ones. The more things change – as the Babu might well have observed – *plus c'est la même chose*.

With so much of it inspired by actual people and places, the dividing line between the real and the imaginary in *Kim* is always very narrow. Some of the characters, the Babu among them, seemed so convincing to me at times as to be real. In Ferozepur, where Kim's mother died of cholera, I found myself momentarily wondering where she was buried, and whether Kim's broken-hearted, opium-sodden father lay beside her, or rested in a pauper's grave somewhere in Lahore. And when I was in Lahore I wondered, too, what became of the half-caste woman who ran a second-hand furniture shop 'by the square where the cheap cabs wait' (which I never managed to find), and who supposedly looked after Kim. What must she have thought, I puzzled, when Kim suddenly vanished for ever from her life that day without even telling her that he was going?

A little game I try out on friends who love *Kim* is to ask them which of its characters they would most like to be. My own first choice, I must confess, would be Mahbub Ali, though I greatly envy Colonel Creighton his job. Kipling himself, I have little doubt, would have chosen Kim – that happy, carefree and footloose child whose nursery was the bazaars, alleyways and rooftops of Lahore, and who was free to roam wherever he wanted. For this little Friend of all the World was clearly an idealised and nostalgic recreation of Kipling's own early childhood in India – so soon to be cruelly snatched from him by his removal to England, and five desperately unhappy years with foster-parents. But in his heart, like many of us I suspect, Kipling may also have secretly yearned to be the lama, whom he portrays with such extraordinary tenderness and love, and whom some critics see as the real hero of *Kim*.

To many people, however, the real hero of Kipling's masterpiece is neither Kim nor the lama. It is India itself – 'this fair land of Hind' – to which he owed so much and with which he will always be associated, even if only a fraction of his life was spent there. In *Kim*, with its unsurpassed descriptions of this bewitching and bewildering land, he has repaid that debt a thousandfold.

RUDYARD KIPLING
BORN 30ᵗʰ DEC. 1865
DIED 18ᵗʰ JAN. 1936

# CHRONOLOGY

| | |
|---|---|
| 1857–8 | Indian Mutiny |
| 1857 | Siege of Lucknow |
| 1865 | Rudyard Kipling born, Bombay, December 30 |
| 1871–7 | Rudyard and sister Trix left in Southsea, England, with foster parents |
| 1878–80 | Second Afghan War. Roberts occupies Kabul |
| 1882 | Rudyard returns to India, starts work on *Civil and Military Gazette*, Lahore |
| 1885 | Visits Khyber Pass to report talks between Emir of Afghanistan and Viceroy. Also works on *Mother Maturin*, his unpublished novel, which he later draws on for *Kim* |
| 1887 | Moves to Allahabad *Pioneer* |
| 1889 | Leaves India for good |
| 1890 | Russophobic short story 'The Man Who Was' published |
| 1892 | First conceives idea of *Kim*, but shelves it |
| 1893 | Lockwood Kipling leaves India for good |
| 1894 | New museum, on which work had begun in 1890, opens in Lahore, replacing old 'Wonder House' described in *Kim* |
| 1898 | Russophobic poem 'The Truce of the Bear' first published |
| 1901 | *Kim* published |

1907        Kipling awarded Nobel Prize for Literature, then its youngest-ever recipient, and the first British writer to receive it

1936        Death of Kipling, and interment in Westminster Abbey

1947        Indian independence and partition, leading to inter-ethnic massacres on either side of new frontier

Some of those who helped me in my quest have already been acknowledged in this narrative. However, I would also like to thank the following for various assistance: Trixie Schreiber, Honorary Librarian of the Kipling Society; Elizabeth Inglis, librarian responsible for the Kipling manuscripts at Sussex University; Merilyn Hywel-Jones and other members of the British Association for Cemeteries in South Asia; Barrie McManmon, who put me in touch with Stephen Brookes; and, as always, my wife Kath, who helped in so many ways – as, too, did my painstaking and eagle-eyed editor, Gail Pirkis.